Formation For Priestly Celibacy:
A Resource Book

Rev. Thomas W. Krenik, D. Min.

Forward by
Most Rev. Harry J. Flynn

The Saint Paul Seminary
School of Divinity
of the University of St. Thomas

St. Paul, MN
1999

NATIONAL CATHOLIC EDUCATIONAL ASSOCIATION

Copyright©1999
ISBN 1-55833-228-6

Cover art by Keith Warrick
Design by Beatriz Ruiz

PLEASE NOTE

This book has a number of references to Pope Paul VI's encyclical on Priestly Celibacy entitled: *Sacerdotalis Caelibatus*. That encyclical is not included as an appendix to this book.

Access this reference through the Internet:

www.vatican.va
The Holy Father
Paul VI
Encyclicals
Sacerdotalis Caelibatus

Acknowledgements

Grateful acknowledgement is made for permission to reproduce the following:

1. Commitment to celibacy in the ordination ritual for deacons
    Excerpts from the English translation of *Ordination of Deacons, Priests and Bishops* © 1975, International Committee on English in the Liturgy, Inc. All rights reserved.

2. Continuum of Human Sexuality and Reflection on Sexuality Continuum
    © Patricia H. Livingston, Livingston Associates, 2 Adalia Avenue #501, Tampa, FL 33606

3. Canons 247.1, 247.2, 277.1, 277.2, 277.3, 599
    Code of Canon Law, Latin-English Edition (Washington, D.C.: Canon Law Society of America, 1983)

4. "The Living Flame of Love" by St. John of the Cross
    From *The Collected Works of St. John of the Cross* translated by Kieran Kavanaugh and Otilio Rodriguez © 1979, 1991, by Washington Province of Discalced Carmelites. ICS Publications 2131 Lincoln Road, N.E. Washington, D.C. 20002 U.S.A.

5. *Celibacy: A Way to Love* by Archbishop Harry J. Flynn, D.D.
    Reprinted with permission of the author

I am grateful to Fr. Mark Dosh, Fr. Robert Schwartz, Sr. Katarina Schuth, O.S.F., and Rev. Valerie Strand who read the manuscript and offered many helpful observations and recommendations.

The Holy Trinity (Andrei Rublev)
Russian icon, dated 1411

Foreword

In 1990 an opportunity was presented that I will long remember and not easily forget. I was invited by our Holy Father, John Paul II, to participate in the Synod of 1990, dedicated to the subject of formation of priests in the circumstances of the present day. Having an opportunity to participate in a world-wide Synod on any subject of interest to the Church is, in my judgment, an opportunity which should be given to every bishop. It gives the participant a deep insight into the universality of the Church.

At the Synod I heard many interventions given by bishops on various subjects concerning the formation of men to the priesthood. Among these interventions the subject of celibacy was frequently presented. It was interesting to note that it was, indeed, a value which so many looked upon as a gift of the Church.

As a result of that Synod our Holy Father, John Paul II, gave the Church the apostolic exhortation, *Pastores Dabo Vobis*. In that splendid exhortation the Holy Father once more affirmed the centuries-old choice which the western Church has made and maintained, despite all the difficulties and objections raised down the centuries, of conferring the order of presbyter only on men who have given proof that they have been called by God to the gift of chastity in absolute and perpetual celibacy. The Holy Father stated the importance of presenting and explaining celibacy in the fullness of its biblical, theological and spiritual richness, as a precious gift given by God to His Church. It is a sign of the Kingdom which is not of this world, a sign of God's love for the world and of the undivided love of the priest for God and God's people. When they are presented in this way, celibacy will be seen as a positive enrichment of the priesthood.

The fourth edition of the Program of Priestly Formation, issued by the Bishops of the United States in November, 1992, states: "Nothing less than a coordinated and multi-faceted program of instruction, dialogue, and encouragement will aid seminarians to understand the nature and purpose of celibate chastity and to embrace it wholeheartedly in their lives. Sexuality finds its authentic meaning in relation to mature love. Seminarians should understand the connection between mature love and celibacy. In doing so, the insights of modern psychology can be of a considerable aid. The goal of psychosexual, social, and spiritual development should be to form seminarians into chaste celibate men who are loving pastors of the people they serve." #287

Father Thomas W. Krenik, in this marvelous work, *Formation for Priestly Celibacy: A Resource Book*, has written out of his years of experience as Spiritual Director at The Saint Paul Seminary in St. Paul, Minnesota. He has focused upon seven elements which he perceives to be essential in meeting the challenge for formation in celibacy: 1) internalization of presbytal values; 2) pattern of contemplative prayer; 3) capacity for solitude; 4) age-appropriate psychosexual development; 5) capacity for intimacy in human relationships; 6) experience of community support; and 7) accountability to others. Father Krenik writes splendidly and comprehensively, and as a result his work would be of great assistance to any formator who has that great responsibility of presenting and explaining celibacy as a precious gift given by God to His Church.

In my judgment Father Krenik himself has made an inestimable gift to the Church in the work, *Formation for Priestly Celibacy: A Resource Book.* I strongly believe that this work will be very helpful to every formator involved in walking with men who are preparing for the priesthood in our present day and age. I take this opportunity to thank him for this work and I wholeheartedly encourage others to use it.

Most Reverend Harry J. Flynn, D.D.
Archbishop of Saint Paul and Minneapolis

September 1, 1998

Preface

"I remind you to stir into flame the gift of God that you have through the imposition of my hands. For God did not give us a spirit of cowardice but rather of power and love and self-control" (II Tim 1:6-7).

Celibacy is a charism, a gift of God given to some for faithful and loving service in the Church. Ordained ministry is a charism, a gift of God given to some for faithful and loving service in the Church. These two charisms are woven together in the life and ministry of the Church's priests and bishops. Like all *charismata*, they need to be stirred into flame—the flame of life-giving love. The ability to stir these gifts into flame demands a generous heart, an enlightened faith, and exemplary virtue.

This book is compiled primarily for seminarians at the theologate level to aid them in their initial and ongoing formation for priestly celibacy. It may also be helpful for college and pre-theology seminarians, men who are discerning a call to celibacy and priesthood, and priests who want to re-visit the meaning and value of priestly celibacy in their own lives in the spirit of the final chapter of *Pastores Dabo Vobis* (I Remind You To Rekindle the Gift of God That Is Within You) and *Equipped for the Work of Ministry: A Reflection and Planning Guide for the Continuing Formation of Priests* (NCCB, 1996).

This volume is designed as a resource book, a workbook, for students and their formators. It begins with my essay detailing seven guiding principles for a program of formation for priestly celibacy that are derived from theology, spirituality, and psychology. Appendices and work sheets are designed to be used in formation sessions and in private reflection. I have included the text of Archbishop Harry Flynn's presentation given during the 1990 Synod of Bishops and the encyclical letter *Sacerdotalis Caelibatus* of Pope Paul VI. A number of books that I have found helpful are listed in a bibliography.

The inspiration of this book comes from many people. The immediate source is the seminarians whom I am privileged to serve and accompany at The Saint Paul Seminary since 1989. Their persistence in desiring quality and substantial assistance in preparation for a commitment to life-long celibacy has motivated me to re-examine the Church's vision of priestly celibacy in ecclesial documents, the insights of modern psychology concerning the dynamics of psycho-sexual development, and the qualities of spirituality in diocesan priesthood. This task would not have been possible without the cooperation of my co-workers in our Spiritual Formation Department, past and present. They include Sr. Paul Therese Saiko, SSND, Frs. Ron

Bowers, Doug Dandurand, Bill McDonough, Bob Nygaard, Mike Papesh, and Bob Schwartz. Our experience of working together has truly been one of collaboration. I am also grateful for the support and encouragement of my colleague, Sr. Katarina Schuth, OSF.

My participation in The Christian Institute for the Study of Human Sexuality (8901 New Hampshire Ave., Silver Spring, MD 20903, 301-422-5500) under the direction of Fr. James J. Gill, S.J., M.D., was a significant resource in developing this book. The structure of the program includes seminars that consider human sexuality from the perspectives of moral theology, psychology, and spirituality. Sessions titled "Talking About Sex" are designed to help participants become more comfortable talking about all sexual matters and to sharpen counseling skills in this area. Each student meets twice weekly with a tutor to discuss cases and questions, and to process learnings from the seminars and readings. An extensive library provides a good collection of printed, taped, and filmed literature related to sexuality.

Another great resource has been my contact with my confreres in the Federation of Seminary Spiritual Directors, comprised of priests in the United States and Canada who are involved in the ministry of spiritual formation in seminaries. I was privileged to serve as president of this group for two years. We have become a source of personal and professional support to each other on a very significant level. My article *Formation for Priestly Celibacy: Seven Guiding Elements* appeared in an earlier version in *The Journal* of the FSSD in 1996.

My recent sabbatical (Spring semester, 1998) at the Church of the Sacred Heart in Coronado, California, provided necessary time for what I call the three R's: Rest, Reading, and wRiting. I am most grateful to Fr. Michael Murphy, Pastor, Msgr. Jeremiah Sullivan, Fr. John Wheeler, and Sylvia Alvarado for their gracious welcome, hospitality, and prayerful support. My daily walks along the ocean beach contributed to a quieting of my mind and heart in order to let the good Spirit guide me (Ps 143).

I am grateful to Fr. James J. Walsh, Executive Director of the Seminary Department of the National Catholic Educational Association, for his helpful editorial comments and for arranging the publication of this material.

Finally, I express my gratitude to my ordinary, Archbishop Harry J. Flynn. I am encouraged by his affirmation of me and my work and I am continually inspired by the strength of his shepherding after the heart of Christ. I thank him for writing the forward and for his permission to include his article, *Celibacy: A Way of Love*, in this resource book.

Rev. Thomas W. Krenik
Spiritual Director and Director of Spiritual Formation
The Saint Paul Seminary

May 31, 1998 *Pentecost*

Formation for Priestly Celibacy: Seven Guiding Elements

These pages are designed to assist seminarians and their formators in the process of cultivating an appreciation for and making a life-long commitment to priestly celibacy. It provides resources to reverently stir into flame this gift of God in the Church. Ecclesial documents, insights of modern psychology, and the qualities of spirituality in diocesan priesthood are the sources of these guiding principles.

Questions after each section are designed for personal reflection. They may suggest topics for conversation with a spiritual director, friend, or another confidant.

Introduction

Bachelorhood, consecrated virginity, the religious vow of celibacy, priestly celibacy—these are four different lifestyles for single persons to follow Christ. They are four different ways to live the Christian virtue of chastity. The virtue of chastity takes another form in the sacrament of matrimony.

Priestly celibacy is called a "brilliant jewel," a "sweet and heavy burden," and a "grave, ennobling obligation" by Pope Paul VI[1]. The teaching of Vatican II locates its discussion of priestly celibacy within the context of perfect and perpetual continence for the sake of the kingdom of heaven. "[It] has always been held in especially high esteem by the church as a feature of priestly life. For it is at once a sign of pastoral charity and an incentive to it as well as being in a special way a source of spiritual fruitfulness in the world."[2]

How does the priest experience celibacy this way? How do his parishioners experience his celibacy? How is a seminarian formed in the Church's vision for priestly celibacy? How is he prepared to sustain his commitment to celibate chastity, indeed perfect and perpetual continence, in light of the inevitable challenges in his intrapsychic realities and interpersonal encounters? The following three vignettes begin to concretize and illustrate the challenges for seminarians, seminary faculty, and diocesan personnel.

Fritz[3] is a 25 year old student in his third year of theology. He recently called his spiritual director to set up a special appointment. He appeared anxious when he arrived and immediately began talking about how confused and upset he was. In his teaching parish there is a drop-in center for youth. Fritz has been counseling a fourteen year old boy who has been in a lot of trouble at school. This past week Fritz felt like he was beginning to make progress. The boy shared how he had been beaten regularly by his father. His mother had died when he was an infant. For the first time, Fritz felt like he had earned the confidence of the youngster. As the boy shared some of the pain of his life, Fritz saw tears well up in the boy's eyes. He immediately went up and hugged the boy. As he did so, he began to cry himself. He then realized the intense emotion he felt and was aware that he was experiencing an erection. Fritz felt himself being pulled. On the one hand he wanted to put as much distance as possible between himself and the boy. On the other hand he wanted to just hold him. Fritz thinks that he is heterosexual but isn't sure. Any sexual attraction he has experienced before has been toward people about his own age. There are many questions that run through his head: Am I a pedophile? Should I leave the seminary? Is it possible that I was abused as a child and don't remember it? What does this incident mean?

Chuck is a 43 year old man who is in his second year of theology. He studies hard and gets good grades. He is quite concerned about orthodoxy and feels it is important to denounce any of his fellow students who question the magisterium. He openly states that it is his desire to be a "traditional" priest; he is angry with clergy, especially faculty members, whom he believes have drifted into laxity. He maintains an uncompromising horarium of prayers and devotions. He admits that he has had numerous sexual relations with women in the past, but has not desired to become involved in any committed relationship with a woman. Being celibate, he purports, will be no problem whatsoever for him. He is trying arduously to rid himself of masturbation and of fantasizing about having sex with women. He sees these as disgusting flaws in his striving for perfection. He is clear that women are best serving God by being mothers and by knowing their place of service in the Church. Many of Chuck's classmates choose to distance themselves from him. They are intimidated by him and are afraid that they will be the target of what they perceive to be massive rage and vindictive behavior toward them.

Arnie is a 33 year old seminarian beginning his first year of theology. During his admissions interview he told the board members that he is gay and that he has been sexually abstinent for the past two years. Arnie admits to his spiritual director that on some weekends he goes to gay bars with some friends and sometimes he watches pornographic videos. He is angry that "even my own Church considers me a disordered person." Arnie is fearful that he may eventually test HIV positive.

These three vignettes raise a number of questions in addition to the ones mentioned earlier. How should spiritual directors, formation advisors, and other faculty members work with these students? Would Fritz, Chuck, and Arnie remain faithful as celibate priests? What are the Church's expectations about the behavior and attitudes around sexuality for seminarians? How much should vocation directors, rectors, and bishops know about a priesthood candidate's behavior and attitudes regarding human sexuality and celibacy? What are essential elements for a helpful and integrated program of formation for celibate chastity?

In response to the desire expressed in the encyclical letter *On Priestly Celibacy* that appropriate instructions be issued to help those who have the serious responsibility of preparing future priests for a life of sacerdotal celibacy, *A Guide to Formation in Priestly Celibacy* was published in 1974. The latter document names four tasks in formation for priestly celibacy. "It is the educator's task, therefore, to cultivate in his students an appreciation for the gift of celibacy, a disposition for its acceptance, a recognition of its presence, and its practice."[4]

This guiding document asserts that celibacy is "a value, a grace, a charism, [that] has to be presented in its true light if it is to be appreciated, chosen, and genuinely lived."[5] An authentic and viable understanding of celibacy is necessary. "Priestly celibacy is not simply to be identified with remaining unmarried or with sexual continence. It is a renunciation of three natural tendencies: genital function, conjugal love, and natural fatherhood, made 'for the love of the kingdom of heaven.' To be a genuine and sincere witness to religious values, it can never be a negation of, or a flight from, sex, but rather it must be the sublimation of sexuality."[6] Sublimation may be described as the process of awareness and acceptance of sexual feelings and channeling the sexual energy to activity judged to be "higher" culturally, socially, physically, aesthetically, or spiritually.

An enlightened program of training for priestly celibacy will take into account all the aims of seminary formation. Since *Pastores Dabo Vobis* and the fourth edition of the *Program of Priestly Formation* were promulgated, we have come to name them as human, spiritual, intellectual, and pastoral formation. Woven into this comprehensive program of formation will be the specific elements necessary for training in priestly celibacy.

This formational endeavor presupposes and implies that seminarians will be at the same time formed as men, as Christians, and as priests. A program of formation for priestly celibacy must have three aims or levels of formation, answering the need to form personalities that are integrally human, Christian, and priestly. In each of these three areas, the document from the Congregation describes the necessary formation in human maturity, emotional maturity, sexual maturity, and self-control.[7]

In light of the Church's vision and general guiding principles, I have formulated seven elements that I perceive to be essential in initial and ongoing formation for priestly celibacy. They are: internalization of presbyteral values; pattern of contemplative prayer; capacity for solitude; age-appropriate psychosexual development; capacity for intimacy in human friendships; experience of community support; and accountability to others. In this article I will develop each of these seven areas.

Christian marriage and celibacy share the same spiritual goal, to be life-giving and love-giving. "I came that they might have life, and have it more abundantly"

(Jn 10:10).[8]   "This is my commandment: love one another as I love you. No one has greater love than this, to lay down one's life for one's friends" (Jn 15:12-13). All of God's people are called to the fullness of this life and love.   Celibacy has a distinct process and path to this goal. A celibacy formation program must be based on "integrative knowledge and transformational techniques."[9]   For the priesthood candidate this means possessing an accurate understanding of sexuality and celibacy, being psychosexually mature, and demonstrating the ability to sublimate his sexual desires towards pastoral service in the Church.   I believe that the following seven guiding elements embodied in a formation program foster both the necessary sexual integration and the transcendental motivation that priestly celibacy demands.

I. Internalization of Presbyteral Values

The Context of Spirituality in Diocesan Priesthood

The Church calls to the ordained priesthood men who are committed to the celibate lifestyle. We see this reflected in the rite of ordination of deacons in which the public promise of a commitment to celibacy happens liturgically before the ordination itself. This signals that the discernment by a candidate and by the Church about a particular candidate's readiness for a life of celibate chastity is distinct from and prior to the discernment about readiness for ministerial priesthood.

At the same time, celibacy must be understood and experienced in the whole context of spirituality in diocesan priesthood. "Wholesome priestly spirituality embraces prayer, simplicity of life, obedience, pastoral service, and celibate chastity."[10] These key presbyteral values are interrelated and are experienced as developmental and dynamic as a person progresses in formation and in priesthood. Just as a person's prayer life deepens and matures throughout his life, so his experience of celibate chastity can be expected to mature as he progresses in life and ministry.[11] "For an adequate priestly spiritual life, celibacy ought not to be considered and lived as an isolated or purely negative element, but as one aspect of a positive, specific and characteristic approach to being a priest."[12] Celibate chastity and the other values of priestly spirituality must be internalized and appropriated as meaningful and life-giving experiential realities.

For the priesthood candidate this means that he must sense an interior call to the celibate lifestyle and at the same time be attracted to the whole context of spirituality in diocesan priesthood. For seminary formators this means that they must see evidence of the ability to sustain a life pattern of chaste celibacy in the candidate and it is their duty to present all the values of presbyteral spirituality in a way that is formative and transformative for the priesthood candidate.

Priestly celibacy is not an intelligible sign if it is seen in isolation. "The promotion and defense of priestly celibacy cannot be carried on in isolation from other aspects of the priest's life and ministry. If there is a relation, as we believe, among celibacy, community, authority, and faith itself, then a crisis in one area is bound to affect the others."[13] Prayer, simplicity of life, obedience, pastoral service, and celibate chastity are interrelated forms of availability to God, the Church, and the poor. They are all part of a radical way of living according to the Gospel.

In reflecting on priestly spirituality, a notable feature of *Pastores Dabo Vobis* is that it relates the evangelical counsels of obedience, celibacy, and poverty to the witness of a priest's life and ministry.[14] The priest's way of life and way of serving is modelled on the life and ministry of Christ. In obedience a priest cooperates with his bishop and fellow priests in serving the diocese. The celibate state makes him available for a total love of the whole flock. By living simply a priest is ready to embrace the type and place of ministry where there is a need. This way of life is the kind of seamless garment of Christ that a priest must put on himself. It is an outward garment that reflects an undivided heart formed by these gospel and priestly values. "For all of you who were baptized into Christ have clothed yourselves with Christ" (Gal 3:27).

The obligation of priestly celibacy must become "the candidate's own accepted personal obligation under the influence of divine grace and with full reflection and liberty, and evidently not without the wise and prudent advice of spiritual directors who are concerned not to impose the choice, but rather to dispose the candidate to become more conscious in his choice."[15] This approach will bring an interior sense of joy, peace, and freedom about the commitment to celibacy made for the love of Christ.

This does not preclude the possibility that a seminarian or priest will experience some ambivalence, mixed feelings, struggles, or even failures in the living out of these presbyteral values. Rather, each person must honestly face his struggles and challenges, taking responsibility for his own issues and needs. This entails living through the reality of his experience with his mind and heart set on the value and commitment. The remainder of this section focuses on the presbyteral value of celibacy.

Discerning the Charism of Celibacy

The understanding of celibacy as a charism is rooted in Scripture. In Pauline theology both marriage and celibacy seem to be viewed in the light of spiritual gifts. "Each has a particular gift [charisma] from God, one of one kind and one of another" (I Cor 7:7). Those who choose to be married and those who choose celibacy "receive a gift from God, his own gift, that is, the grace proper to this choice, to this way of living, to this state."[16] The gift received is "a true gift from God, one's own gift, intended for concrete persons. It is specific, that is, suited to their vocation in life."[17]

The gift or charism of celibacy that is given is not so much something that God gives a person, like a special talent. Rather, it is the grace for a way of being, a particular modality of a person's graced existence, a graced way of being. It is an intrinsic part of one's identity. Deep down in one's heart a person comes to realize this truth at the very core of what it means for him to be who he is. This kind of recognition of one's identity as a celibate person demands careful discernment that includes honest soul-searching and candid feedback from people who know him well. "Celibacy leads to a way of being, not of functioning."[18] Celibacy is part of what it means to be a priest. It is a way of being with people that is life-giving and love-giving.

Discernment about one's celibate identity taps into "that peak experience in our evolving vocational consciousness during which we undergo our calling in terms of an existential inability to become otherwise."[19] This existential inability to do otherwise is a biblical intuition going back to Christ. "Some are incapable of marriage because they were born so; some, because they were made so by others; some, because they have renounced marriage for the sake of the kingdom of heaven. Whoever can accept this ought to accept it" (Mt 19:12). Some translations render the Greek *eunouchia* more literally as "eunuchs."

Schillebeeckx points out that this text does not speak of the unmarried (*agamoi*), but of the unmarriageable (*eunouchoi*), those not suited for marriage. The unpleasant sounding word "eunuch," existentially incapable of marriage, indicates one of many distinguishing characteristics of Jesus and his disciples. They are so grasped by Christ Jesus (Phil 3:12) and the reality of the Kingdom of God and they are so graced to discover the full overpowering hidden wealth of God's reign that they could not existentially do other than leave everything and follow him. For them it was an experience of the inner logic of their enthusiastic discovery of what we so often speak of as "for the sake of the kingdom of heaven."[20]

Schillebeeckx asserts that in the Gospels celibacy is not an abstract ideal nor an imposition nor a desideratum. "Jesus approvingly states a fact of religious psychology: in view of their joy on finding the 'hidden pearl' (Mk 4:11), some people cannot do other than live unmarried. This religious experience itself makes them unmarriageable, actually incapable of marriage; their heart is where their treasure is."[21] In another Gospel passage it is said, "Whoever can accept this ought to accept it" (Mt 19:12). The Greek verb *choreo* in this sentence means to make room, to receive or hold, to yield in accordance with. "If the vocation of celibacy has been given to you, yield to it. For ultimately, you can best become yourself in Christ by living in accordance with the way he is calling you."[22]

Coombs and Nemeck discuss two essential characteristics of the celibate vocation implied in the latter part of Matthew 19:12. First, the person called is not only able to be celibate but specifically enabled to be a celibate person. It is not so much a matter of whether one can be celibate, but rather that one receives the ability to be celibate. It is God who causes and provides the capability. One's unmarriageability is then a necessary effect of having been called by God to celibacy. Second, the main verb in this phrase (Mt 19:12) is in the imperative mood. This indicates that having received a vocation to celibacy, the person is impelled from within to move in that direction.[23] This life-direction or "vocational imperative" flows from and is shaped by one's personal encounter with Christ.

> A vocational imperative to celibacy is at the same time spiritual, ontological and moral. It is a *spiritual imperative* because it is an irresistible movement toward God produced by the Spirit in the deepest recesses of our spirit. As such, it penetrates every facet of our spiritualization. It is also an *ontological imperative* because it is an existential inability to be otherwise. In the realm of being, we best become our transformed selves by way of celibacy. It is furthermore a *moral imperative* because it is an inability to become and to do otherwise. Our lifestyle and our behavior emanate from who God is calling us to be.[24]

For the priesthood candidate and those who work with him in discernment and formation it is important to look for signs of this spiritual, ontological, and moral imperative. These signs include an inner peacefulness about actually living as a chaste celibate person and a recognizable ease and comfortable way of relating with people that is loving and life-giving. Another sign is being attracted to spending the bulk of one's life and energy serving others in pastoral charity. Another sign is the ability to sustain a pattern of prayer in the midst of pastoral ministry. Still another sign is the way the candidate speaks about his relationship with Christ and being caught up in the reign of God. Is it evident that he has seen and heard and looked upon and touched the Word of life (see I Jn 1:1-4)?

Some candidates will experience and manifest this vocational imperative for celibacy. For others it will not be as clear. They will need to trust the Church's intuition and lived tradition that, although celibacy is not demanded of the priesthood by its very nature, it is highly meaningful for and in harmony with priesthood. In the celibate state they *"more readily* join themselves to [Christ] with an undivided heart and dedicate themselves *more freely* in Him and through Him to the service of God and of men and women. They are *less encumbered* in their service of His kingdom and of the task of heavenly regeneration (emphasis mine)."[25] For these candidates it means making an inner commitment to voluntarily accept celibacy and devoting themselves to it. By actually living celibacy, an interior conviction may continue to grow. It also means being self-reflective about their intrapsychic and relational experience and receiving feedback from other people, for example, seminary formators, good friends, and people in their parish placement. Are the signs mentioned above present? Are there signs of growing in accepting celibacy? This is, perhaps, the meaning of "specified periods of experimentation" ("preliminary trial period" in another translation) in Pope Paul VI's encyclical.[26]

Schillebeeckx speaks about those who desire to be a priest but do not possess the spontaneous effect of being overwhelmed by the discovery of God's reign. "Because the ministry inwardly calls one to celibacy—which only forces itself upon those who experience the overwhelming discovery of the kingdom of God, for example, the Apostles—the Church imposes the 'spontaneous effect' of that experience on anyone who wants to become a priest, but, perhaps, possesses this experience only in germ as yet, in order that *within it* and *by means of it* he will come indeed to a true religious experience."[27] By voluntarily accepting celibacy one devotes himself to it with full confidence in God's grace, asking to come under the spell of God's kingdom in such a way that existentially celibacy becomes the only possible vocation. This is an action of the will, an act of faith.

Schillebeeckx concludes this section in his work:

> Thus if the church recognizes a law of celibacy for priests, this law is only the juridical translation of an anthropological pattern, functioning on the basis of the original experience of an apostle of Christ who, overwhelmed by finding the "hidden treasure," has become blind to the objectively still open possibility

of married life. The law of celibacy is the juridical exponent of the inner logic of a deep religious experience which the church's ministers above all should show in their actual life. The law of celibacy is the church's attempt to *reactivate* the reception of holy orders into that original experience which intrinsically calls forth the spontaneous practice of celibacy.[28]

It is helpful to keep in mind the rich meaning of "law" in the Catholic Church. The purpose of the Code of Canon Law is to create an order in the Church that facilitates the organic development of faith, grace, charisms, and charity in the life of the Church and of the faithful.[29] The Code is founded on Scripture and Tradition. It reflects the doctrine and ecclesiology of the Second Vatican Council. It embodies the Church's dogmatic, liturgical, and moral theology. All of these dynamics are contained in the law of clerical celibacy.

Priesthood candidates who possess the vocational imperative for celibacy can cooperate with God's gift. Candidates who sense that they do not possess this charism can ask God for the gift. Those who are ambivalent or unsure need to engage in careful discernment. The book *Discerning Vocations to Marriage, Celibacy and Singlehood* by Coombs and Nemeck is a very helpful resource in this regard. Those who clearly do not possess the charism of celibacy will do themselves and the Church a great service when they surrender to this reality, discontinue study for priesthood, and honor their authentic vocational imperative.

Celibacy in the Context of Chastity

Appropriating the value of priestly celibacy includes understanding and practicing the moral virtue of chastity. The practice of chastity refers to the adoption of moral and religious norms that moderate and regulate the sexual appetite in both personal and social circumstances.[30] All Christians are called to this evangelical imperative that entails appreciating, integrating, and ordering our sexuality.[31] It challenges us to encounter the relational power of our sexuality and to use our sexual energies to foster friendships and other relationships of love and service. Personal awareness and ownership of our sexual feelings are key in bringing order and harmony to this dynamic dimension of our identity. Awareness and acceptance help us to realize the choices we have regarding how we want to channel our sexual energy.

Chastity is not simply suppressing sexual thoughts and desires and avoiding sexual activity. It "consists in the long-term integration of one's thoughts, feelings, and actions in a way that values, esteems, and respects the dignity of oneself and others. Chastity frees us from the tendency to act in a manipulative or exploitive manner in our relationships and enables us to show true love and kindness always."[32]

To be chaste means to place one's sexual appetites within proper relationship to one's other appetites, reason, and will. This posture is achieved by taking into account not only the well-being and needs of oneself, but also the overall good of society. Chastity and sexuality are not merely one's private domain; they must be integrated into the larger social reality and environment. Chastity is not the neglect of one's sexual faculties, but reflective and compassionate interaction with other people.[33] These social and affective dimensions of human sexuality are manifested in a person's capacity to relate with emotional warmth, compassion, and tenderness.

Chastity is the foundational virtue that provides meaning for the tradition of celibacy in the Church. "Rather than trying to understand chastity from the point of view of celibacy, we need to turn the process around and measure celibacy from the perspective of chastity."[34] This virtue must be the ground on which we seek to build a community of right relationships. Chastity is the virtue that brings both celibate persons and married couples into mutually affirming relationships.

Both married persons and celibate persons are called to the gospel vision of chastity. Both marriage and celibacy draw their meaning from the relational capacity of human beings. Pope John Paul II states that "sexuality is an enrichment of the whole person—body, emotions, and soul—and it manifests its inmost meaning in leading to the gift of self in love."[35] Celibacy and marriage are both ways of living the fundamental gift of human sexuality.

> Sexuality is a relational power, not merely a capacity for performing specific acts. The Vatican Congregation for Catholic Education speaks of sexuality as a "fundamental component of personality, one of its modes of being, of manifestation, of communicating with others, of feeling, of expressing and of living human love." Sexuality prompts each of us from within, calling us to personal as well as spiritual growth and drawing us out from self to interpersonal bonds and commitments with others, both women and men. It includes the qualities of sensitivity, understanding, intimacy, openness to others, compassion, and mutual support.[36]

Our call to gospel chastity is rooted in this understanding of sexuality as the core characteristic of all human beings that leads us beyond ourselves into right relationships with other people. Celibate chastity is one way to experience this natural human yearning for connection with others.

Formation for the virtue of chastity begins in one's family of origin and includes "an apprenticeship in self-mastery which is a training in human freedom."[37] In seminary formation a candidate for priesthood must look again at his experience of chastity to ensure that he is a man of integrity and capable of self-control of his sexual appetite. Under the influence of charity, his practice of chastity is a "school of the gift of the person."[38] Sexual integration and self-mastery are ordered to the gift of the self, enabling a person to give of himself freely and joyfully in pastoral charity. In his book *The Courage to Be Chaste*, Benedict Groeschel provides a helpful discussion of the meaning of the virtue of chastity and pastoral advice for those who struggle to grow in this important Christian virtue.[39]

Would that every man who is about to be ordained a priest could make this statement with honesty and assurance: "Celibate chastity is a meaningful and fulfilling way for me to live my life as a sexual being." The ultimate goal in discernment about celibacy is for the person to discover from experience and deep soul-searching whether celibate chastity is a "fit" for him so that he will be able to make a free and conscious commitment to the celibate lifestyle as part of his life and ministry as a priest. It is essential for the person to internalize and personalize celibate chastity as a value and as a meaningful way to live. He must be able to say, "I am choosing celibate chastity because it allows me to meet my psychological and spiritual needs, to feel close to God, and to serve others," or whatever words express his own rationale for renouncing genital sexual expression, conjugal love, and natural fatherhood for the sake of the Kingdom of God. (See the work sheet on page 66 for an exercise titled "Why Celibacy for Me?" to help facilitate this process.)

To experience celibate chastity for the sake of God's reign and as a source of spiritual fruitfulness that comes from the Holy Spirit, it must be willed and chosen in deep faith. "This faith does not merely show us the kingdom of God in its future fulfillment. It permits us and makes it possible for us to identify ourselves in a special way with the truth and reality of that kingdom . . . [It] bears in itself especially the interior dynamism of the mystery of the redemption of the body . . . [It] is a special participation in the mystery of the redemption (of the body)."[40] This deep foundational faith is formed in the community of the faithful; it is nurtured throughout seminary formation and it continues to grow in the life and ministry of priesthood.

The candidate for priesthood must be able to internalize the value of celibate chastity in the context of all the dimensions of spirituality in diocesan priesthood, including obedience, simplicity of life, pastoral service, and prayer. It is this context that makes *priestly celibacy* distinctive from bachelorhood, consecrated virginity, and the religious vow of celibacy.

Questions for Reflection

1. How does priestly celibacy make sense for you? What is its value for you?
2. In what ways do you perceive that celibacy is an interior call for you?
3. Is the obligation of priestly celibacy your "own accepted personal obligation?"
4. What signs do you see in yourself, and do other people see in you, which indicate that priestly celibacy is a "fit" for you?
5. How do you sublimate your sexual appetite? For what do you sublimate your sexual appetite?

II. Pattern of Contemplative Prayer

In addressing the topic of priestly celibacy the *Program of Priestly Formation* first speaks about the importance of a proper understanding of celibacy and the necessity of internalizing the value of celibacy. Then the role of prayer is mentioned. "A life of prayer and a commitment to serve others are equally indispensable for a healthy and lasting celibate commitment."[41] Priestly celibacy cannot be sustained without an authentic and deep life of prayer. Experience shows that a priest needs the centering role of *contemplative* prayer in his life and ministry.

Contemplative Prayer

I use this term contemplative prayer in two ways. First, contemplation is a kind of prayer that people experience when serious about an established pattern of prayer and progress in virtuous living. A progression usually occurs from vocal prayer to mental prayer to contemplative prayer. This progression may happen within a given prayer experience, for example, from *lectio divina* to *meditatio* to *oratio* to *contemplatio*. Teresa of Avila uses the imagery of four ways of watering a garden to describe four degrees of prayer. They are drawing water from a well (prayer of beginners), turning the crank of a waterwheel with a system of aqueducts (prayer of recollection), channeling water from a river or stream (prayer of quiet), and being soaked in a downpour (prayer of union).[42] When a person is graced with the fourth degree of prayer, God does all the work. Contemplation is resting quietly in God's presence, simply being with the Lord. It is a communion with God that is beyond the need for words. Priestly celibacy is sustained and its spiritual fruitfulness is deepened as one progresses in the experience of being a praying person.

Second, the term contemplation may mean the "simple loving attention to the gift of God's presence and action in human life, history, Church, and world, as well as in human self-expression through those activities by which we seek to participate more fully in establishing an authentic communion among persons."[43] This contemplative posture is intent upon noticing and being present to the transforming and liberating presence of God in the celebration of the Liturgy, in prayerfully being with God's Word, in relationships, in serving others and in being served, in the traces of the paschal mystery found in living a virtuous Christian life. This kind of prayer is "the movement of the attentive human heart to participate in the very life of God, to respond to the myriad ways that God comes in Christ through the power of the Spirit."[44]

Trinitarian Communion

As Pope John Paul II begins his discussion on priestly identity in *Pastores Dabo Vobis*, he teaches that the priest's very identity like every Christian identity, has its roots in the Trinity; and the priest is to have intimate communion with the Blessed Trinity.[45] This focus signals the weight of the foundational truth of the Trinity in Christian spirituality and surely in priestly spirituality. This Trinitarian origin honors the emphasis in the biblical, credal, and liturgical tradition. Our praxis ought to mirror this doctrine.

Priestly spirituality is essentially Trinitarian in its identity and expression. The priest's life and ministry are rooted in and formed by the multiple and rich intercommunion of relationships that arise from the Trinity and are prolonged in the communion of the Church. A priest's experience of prayer leads him deeper into the communion of the Trinity that he may mirror this *communio* in his ministry and in his relationships.

Through their spiritual formation seminarians and priests come to live in "holy, familiar and attentive union with the Father, through his Son Jesus Christ in the Holy Spirit."[46] In contemplative prayer the priest experiences this divine communion, notices it, reflects on it, and rejoices in it. He comes to know the transcendence, immanence, and indwelling presence of God. "Whoever loves me will keep my word, and my Father will love him, and we will come to him and make our dwelling with him" (Jn 14:23). "And I will ask the Father, and he will give you another Advocate to be with you always, the Spirit of Truth . . . [Y]ou know it, because it remains with you, and will be in you" (Jn 14:16-17). "Yet I live, no longer I, but Christ lives in me; insofar as I now live in the flesh, I live by faith in the Son of God who has loved me and given Himself up for me" (Gal 2:20). These biblical truths become embodied in the life and ministry of the priest as more and more he actualizes his baptismal identity and discipleship.

Through contemplative prayer one comes to a "devotional knowledge" of the mystery of the Trinity. Such knowledge, which Ignatius of Loyola would call "felt knowledge," is "the fruit of intimate and personal experience of another rather than the result of study. It is a quest guided by love rather than by intellectual curiosity. This knowledge is received not so much by the mind as by the heart."[47]

I highlight two ways of praying that foster this devotional knowledge of the Trinity. The first is a colloquy with the persons of the Trinity. This way of praying is suggested by Ignatius of Loyola at the end of meditations and contemplations in the *Spiritual Exercises*. St. Ignatius says that the "colloquy is made, properly speaking, in the way one friend speaks to another, or a servant to one in authority—now begging a favor, now accusing oneself for some misdeed, now communicating one's concerns and asking counsel about them."[48] Sometimes this colloquy might lead one simply to be quiet in the presence of the Triune God.

A second way of praying to foster devotional knowledge of the Trinity is to pray with the icon of the Trinity by Andrew Rublev. The open space at the table near the bottom of the icon can only depict an invitation for the one who contemplates the icon to enter into the communion of the Trinity. To pray before this icon is to experience the gentle invitation to enter the mystery of hospitality and intimacy within the holy circle. It is to know the welcome of the three angels by Abraham and Sarah and also God's welcome of the aged couple into the joy of covenant through a son. It is to know the divine design by which God sends us the only Son as a sacrifice for our sins and gives us new life through the Spirit. Praying with this icon leads us into the mystery of God's self-revelation.[49]

The Church of the East has an awareness that through the spiritual likeness of the image, the reality of holiness becomes present in the icon. Thus, the icon becomes an instrument of grace for the praying person. In the practice and posture of this kind of praying, moving deeper into who and how God is, we become transformed and recreated. We begin to see ourselves and to act in a more God-like way. We more naturally relate with people in our friendships and pastoral relationships with respect, inviting them into the same mystery of hospitality and intimacy that we first know with the Triune God.

A priest is at table many times—at pot-luck dinners and funeral luncheons, at committee meetings and staff meetings, presiding at the table of the Word and the table of the Eucharist. As priest he is commissioned to proclaim the Kingdom of God by creating a space of hospitality so that all God's people find a place at The Table. The priest is to be an icon of Trinitarian communion.

Close to the Heart of Christ

A priest must also foster a deep devotional knowledge of the person of Jesus Christ in his contemplative prayer. In sacramental ordination a priest is configured to Jesus Christ as Head and Shepherd of the Church. In his very being and in his ministry he is to embody the pastoral charity of the Good Shepherd, imitating Christ in his self-giving service.[50] *Pastores dabo vobis iuxta cor meum.* So Pope John Paul II begins his apostolic exhortation, quoting the prophet Jeremiah. This prophetic promise of God is fulfilled in the Church through the life and ministry of her priests. They are to be as the very heart of God, the heart of Christ.

What does the heart of God/Christ look like? How does a priest appropriate the heart of Christ? Helpful imagery is found in the Johannine Gospel where the Greek term *kolpos* (heart) is used twice. "No one has ever seen God. The only Son, God, who is at the Father's side, has revealed him" (Jn 1:18). Other translations read "who is close to the Father's heart" (NRSV), or "who is in the bosom of the Father" (RSV). What a beautiful image for us to contemplate. In the scene of the Last Supper the image recurs. "One of his disciples, the one whom Jesus loved, was reclining at Jesus' side" (Jn 13:23), close to his heart, resting in his bosom. Would that each beloved disciple, each priest, often experienced this intimate communion with the Risen Christ in his contemplative prayer.

This kind of prayer might involve praying with an icon of the beloved disciple leaning against Christ or a statue of the Sacred Heart of Jesus. It could be a *lectio divina* or Ignatian contemplation of Gospel passages that portray the compassionate heart of Christ. The goal is very simple: be there. Be with the Lord. Be close to his heart. Share in the "feelings and attitudes of Jesus Christ."[51] Ask to know, love, and serve him in a deeper way.

Pastores Dabo Vobis states that pastoral charity, embodying the heart of Christ, is expressed and replenished by communion with Christ in the Eucharist. Through his celebration of the Eucharist a priest is called and enabled to give his life a sacrificial dimension.[52] This theme resonates with the exhorting words in the homily at the ordination of a priest: "Your ministry will perfect the spiritual sacrifice of the faithful by uniting it to Christ's sacrifice, the sacrifice which is offered sacramentally through your hands. Know what you are doing and imitate the mystery you celebrate." In his daily celebration of the Eucharist the priest is formed and renewed in the sacrificial heart of Christ. This transformation is the fruit of contemplation in the life of the priest.

It can be said that "celibacy is seen as an extension of a priest's celebration of the Eucharist."[53] The 1971 Synod of Bishops spoke of this connection. "Through celibacy the priest, following his Lord, shows in a fuller way his availability, and embarking on the way of the Cross with paschal joy he ardently desires to be consumed in an offering which can be compared with the Eucharist."[54] The *kenosis* or "emptying out" of Christ (See Phil 2:7) is celebrated in the Eucharist, symbolized in the priest's life of celibacy, and manifested as the priest offers his life and ministry for the sake of the Church and the building up of the Kingdom of God.

Spousal imagery is also used to speak of Christ and of the priest. In sacramental ordination the priest is configured to Jesus Christ the Head *and Spouse* of the Church. "The Church, as the Spouse of Jesus Christ, wishes to be loved by the priest in the total and exclusive manner in which Jesus Christ her Head and Spouse loved her. Priestly celibacy, then, is the gift of self *in* and *with* Christ *to* his Church and expresses the priest's service to the Church in and with the Lord."[55] This is another image of Christ for the priest to contemplate and to emulate. As he grows in his experience of Christ's spousal love for him and for the Church, he is more disposed to love others as he has been loved.

"'God is love, and they who abide in love abide in God, and God abides in them' (I Jn 4:16). God has poured out his love in our hearts through the holy Spirit who has been given to us (see Rom 5:5); therefore the first and most necessary gift is charity, by which we love God above all things and our neighbor because of him."[56] The priest experiences this greatest theological virtue as both affective charity and effective charity. Affective charity is his felt knowledge of God's love in the depths of his being, a loving, dynamic *communio* with the Triune God. Effective charity is his particular acts of love towards others and the sacrificial gift of himself in his life of ministry, manifesting Christ's love for the flock in an *"amoris officium."*[57]

Fostering a Contemplative Attitude

In addition to these ways of praying contemplatively, I highlight two ways of fostering a contemplative attitude. The first is through the daily practice of the Consciousness Examen[58] and the second is the Dynamic Memory Exercise.[59]

Consciousness Examen

This prayer exercise, with its five moments of thanksgiving, prayer for enlightenment, review of the day, prayer of contrition, and hopeful resolution for the future, helps a person to become more aware of the presence and action of God in the daily experience of life. Here is a sketch of the examen:

Reflective Thanksgiving: Start with the attitude of thanksgiving. For whom and for what am I particularly grateful this day? Give thanks to God for gifts given and received this day.

Prayer for Enlightenment: Pray that the light of Christ might illuminate the experiences of the day and enlighten your prayerful reflection so that this time of prayer might be a Spirit-guided awareness. Oh Lord, help me to see myself as you see me.

Review of the Day: Prayerfully review the day with God. Allow memories of experiences and encounters to spontaneously come into your consciousness. Pay attention to what you see in them now. Can you see any deeper movements beneath these experiences? A need for nurturance, a tug to forgive someone, or a desire to trust God more deeply is, perhaps, emerging.

Contrition or Sorrow: Allow yourself to feel genuine sorrow for sins and failures. Look for ways to seek forgiveness of self, others, God. Stand before God as a loved sinner. Acknowledge God's power and desire to forgive.

Hopeful Resolve for the Future: Name something specific that you can do that is reflective of your desire to change and grow in holiness. It may involve a behavior, attitude, or relationship. Allow yourself to feel a sense of freedom and newness. God is calling you forward into deeper conversion.

Dynamic Memory Exercise

This exercise is a very helpful tool in appreciating the unique way in which God is present and active in each of our lives. The exercise entails prayerfully allowing one's memory to randomly review the past for peak experiences when a person has known or felt the transformative presence of God in a special way. Reflecting on the memories reveals a recognizable pattern. In the discernment process a person can compare present experiences with the pattern surfaced in this memory exercise to be able to say "It is the Lord!" about authentic movements of God. The exercise has these parts:

1. Take some time to be comfortable and center yourself. Pray for a spirit of openness and receptivity to God's grace.

2. Review your life for peak experiences when you have known God's presence and action in your life in significant ways. This is not a calendar memory, starting from childhood and working up to the present. Rather, allow memories to come spontaneously into your consciousness. Collect them. Make notes for yourself that help you to gather them.

3. Set aside any painful memories that have not been resolved or that evoke strong feelings. You may want to look for ways to enter a process of healing of these painful memories at a later time.

4. Put them in chronological order. Look for recurring themes or recognizable patterns in these various experiences. This collage becomes your own "bible" of collected God-experiences. It may reveal a pattern of how God is present and active in your life in a unique way.

5. See if your dynamic memory exercise leads to a brief phrase or mantra that captures your reflections. It may be "God is continually leading me out of bondage," or "Do not fear, I am with you," or "God is a God of surprises for me."

The posture of contemplative prayer, when it is real and rooted at the center of our being, will lead to an opening and unfolding of our consciousness to an awareness of God and the things of God in our personal lives, in the Church, and in society. Unless celibacy opens us up to a personal and intimate relationship with the living God, we turn in on ourselves and become the embodiment of the very values and conventions we are called to confront. Contemplative prayer helps to assure that we do not experience celibacy merely as a state of being unmarried, free to pursue our own whims, imprisoned in a compulsive drive for adolescent self-gratification.[60]

In his research, Richard Sipe has found that many priests who have "achieved celibacy," that is, those who have successfully negotiated each step of celibate development, devote at least one and a half to two hours daily to prayer.[61] So interwoven are prayer and celibacy that Sipe has learned to always inquire first about the prayer life of a priest when making a clinical assessment. A celibate's prayer life will reveal the capacity, quality, and nature of his relationships with God, self, and others.

Intimacy with God is fostered by attending to our spiritual growth needs. Being deeply rooted in the spiritual life is a *sine qua non* for living the Gospel value of celibate chastity, witnessing with an undivided heart to the human search for God. Prayer is a way to channel our sexual appetite. By staying with the energy in our sexual feelings and desires, we can go deeper into our being where we find meaning and where we are satisfied with God's fullness and the affection of Christ Jesus. We move into the realm of self-transcendence and transformation that is the work of God.

Necessity of Transcendental Motivation

The science of psychology has done a great service in guiding us in the process of being integrated and individuated. This is a necessary foundational process. But the ultimate goal for the Christian life is not self-actualization—as important and essential as this process is; the goal is self-transcendence and transformation. As Jesus fully identified with our human weaknesses and carried these frailties through the hopelessness of death into the new life of resurrection, so we must accept our radical incompleteness and surrender to the One who gives us fullness and newness of life. We must take responsibility for our behavior and its ramifications. We must also acknowledge and enter into the paschal mystery, the divine passage of LIFE.

Configured to Christ, Head and Shepherd of the Church, the priest's life and ministry must be modelled after the Good Shepherd. "I am the good shepherd. A good shepherd lays down his life for the sheep. . . This is why the Father loves me, because I lay down my life in order to take it up again. No one takes it from me, but I lay it down on my own. I have power to lay it down, and power to take it up again" (Jn 10:11, 17-18). The ultimate goal is to lay down one's life for the community. One must also be intentional in taking up one's life; this is the process of formation, integration, and coming to maturity.[62] Our model is "Christ Jesus, himself human, who gave himself as ransom for all" (I Tim 2:5-6).

A commitment to celibacy must be made out of a transcendental motivation, that is, to be moved by the depth and richness of God's love, and to be moved to spend one's life in pastoral charity, in perfect love of Christ and the Church. A person must first experience the attractiveness of Jesus Christ; he must be grasped by Christ Jesus (Phil 3:12). The candidate for priestly celibacy must possess a capacity for a transcendental calling. Then he can respond affirmatively and with all his heart to the bishop's question: in the presence of God and the Church, are you resolved, as a sign of your interior dedication to Christ, to remain celibate for the sake of the kingdom and in lifelong service to God and humankind?

Toward Union with God and Others

Existentially spirituality and sexuality are closely connected with each other. The sexuality of the celibate priest is a means to an end.[63] It orients the priest toward union with God, meaningful friendships, and fruitful pastoral relationships. Our sexuality and our spirituality point us beyond ourselves. "It is not good for the man to be alone" (Gen 2:18). We need meaningful relationships with other people and with God. The priest's experience of contemplative prayer helps him to know, love, and serve the Triune God who is the object of his deepest desire. Prayer also helps him to consider the place of relationships in his life.

Both sexuality and spirituality are attentive to the human experience of desire. We learn about our sexuality by paying attention to our sexual desires. They show us the implications of our gender, the degree of our sexual drive, the objects of our sexual excitation, and our sexual orientation.[64] Our sexual desires are intimately connected with our identity. Sexual desire is a metaphor of the mystics. Deep union with God is often described in sexual imagery. A good example of this is "The Living Flame of Love" by John of the Cross: songs of the soul in the intimate communication of loving union with God.

1. O living flame of love
that tenderly wounds my soul
in its deepest center! Since
now you are not oppressive,
now consummate! if it be your will:
tear through the veil of this sweet encounter!

2. O sweet cautery,
O delightful wound!
O gentle hand! O delicate touch
that tastes of eternal life
and pays every debt!
In killing you changed death to life.

3. O lamps of fire!
in whose splendors
the deep caverns of feeling,
once obscure and blind,
now give forth, so rarely, so exquisitely,
both warmth and light to their Beloved.

4. How gentle and lovingly
you wake in my heart,
where in secret you dwell alone;
and in your sweet breathing,
filled with good and glory,
how tenderly you swell my heart with love.[65]

The first words spoken by Jesus in the Johannine Gospel are "What are you looking for?" (Jn 1:38) What do you desire? Near the end of the Gospel the question of Jesus is nuanced: "Whom are you looking for?" (Jn 20:15) Our desires are vocational. They help us to see the direction of the spirit in our lives. Prayer is a place to face and wrestle with our desires. Spiritual direction is a place to receive feedback and guidance in sorting out the meaning of our deep desires.

In this section we have considered the vital role of an established pattern of contemplative prayer in a life of priestly celibacy. I contend that a diocesan priest must be a contemplative-in-action. A life of deep prayer with a posture of attentiveness to the traces of God's presence and action must be the wellspring of one's pastoral service in the Church. This demands that one regularly enter the Trinitarian space of hospitality in the Liturgy of the Church and in personal prayer. A priest must embody the contemplative stance, the discerning sense of God that is rooted in prayer precisely within the course of action, of commitment, and of service to the Church and the world.

Questions for Reflection

1. Describe the practice of prayer in your life. In what ways are you drawn to contemplative prayer?
2. How do you experience "devotional knowledge" of the Trinity? How is it formative of your identity?
3. What does it mean for you to draw close to the heart of Christ?
4. "A commitment to celibacy must be made out of a transcendental motivation." What does this mean for you personally?

III. Capacity For Solitude

The Value of Solitude

Priestly celibacy demands that a man have a capacity for solitude. He must be comfortable being alone. He must like himself and learn to live with himself. Deep within each person is a "celibate core,"[66] a sacred center that no other human person touches. This is where the Spirit of God dwells. It is a place of naked solitude. It is the inward desert where we grapple with our demons and dark nights; it is the place where God purifies our hearts and transforms our desires. It teaches us the importance of solitary time so we can connect with other people in authentic solidarity.

The Gospels portray a Jesus who is comfortable with solitude. He frequently went off to the desert or to a mountain to be alone. He fasted for forty days and forty nights in the desert. He embraced his anguish and agony on the Mount of Olives even as his disciples slept. In teaching about prayer he instructed his disciples "when you pray, go to your inner room, close the door, and pray to your Father in secret" (Mt 6:6). The inner room in a first century Palestinian house would be comparable to our pantry or bedroom in the back of the house.

Solitude fosters the depth of one's identity, a depth that imitates the full stature of Christ. In solitude one receives the healing mercy of our gracious God to deal with personal growth issues and to accept things that cannot be changed. This can only lead to greater interior freedom and a serenity that energizes one for authentic friendships and helpful ministry.

Celibacy leaves an empty space, a void, that demands attention. This space of unfilled longing could become cluttered with images of false gods that give rise to self-indulgent behavior, eccentric isolation, and inappropriate withdrawal from healthy social interaction.[67] When the solitude of life is "more boldly and courageously encountered and embraced, the egotistical deceptions of false unity, false security, and false relationships are dismantled to reveal the ultimate and final celibate option: to surrender to the terrible oneness of the God of infinite mystery, the unknown and unknowable God of infinite possibility."[68] Solitude provides the time and space to face our limits and to face the reality of our utter dependence on God.

A Way Into the Paschal Mystery

The capacity to be alone provides us with a process to deal with the feelings of frustration, anxiety, sadness, and pressure. It is a three-fold dynamic of acknowledging the reality of the feeling, identifying and clarifying the nature of the feeling, and bearing the feeling, sitting with it, living with it.[69] This must be a conscious and deliberate experience, paying attention to the feeling and the experience of embracing the feeling.

The issue of mourning and grieving the losses involved during a lifetime of celibacy is a critical factor that needs careful and positive explanation.[70] The celibate person renounces three very good things: genital sexual activity, conjugal love, and natural fatherhood. This renunciation requires one to let go of these human goods and to realize what one is leaving behind. This is a process that must be lived; the feelings of loss and grief must be acknowledged, identified, and carried.

The living and carrying of these feelings does not mean dwelling on the losses in an unnecessarily morbid or somber way. Rather, it means entering into the paschal nature of the experience. "If anyone wishes to come after me, he must deny himself and take up his cross daily and follow me. For whoever wishes to save his life will lose it, but whoever loses his life for my sake will save it" (Lk 9:23-24). This journey might have noticeable stages similar to the stages of grief identified by Elisabeth Kubler-Ross: denial and isolation, anger, bargaining, depression, and acceptance.

At various times in one's journey different losses will be "front burner" issues. At one time it is the realization "I will never have sexual relations with another human being." At another time it is owning the loss that "I will never have a wife or significant other to grow old with." At other times it will be the reality that "I will never have children to nurture and love" or "I will never be a grandfather." These are very real losses. They hurt. They must be felt and lived as embodied realities. They must be expressed and shared with appropriate persons.

How does one know when he has successfully borne these feelings? What signals indicate that he has embraced the paschal mystery? This only occurs when one has moved from a sense of *loss* to a sense of *gift*, when one can praise and thank God in the given situation. Then the losses are "paschalized." The psalms of lament, which comprise the largest group of psalm-types in the Psalter, are excellent examples of this kind of progression (for example, Psalms 13, 22, 59, 79). The Psalmist moves through expressions of distress and lament to praise of God. This paschal experience is a time to identify with Christ. Praying with the Passion Narratives or transfiguration story (where Moses and Elijah spoke with Jesus about his passage, his exodus, [Luke 9:31]) may help one to move deeper into the paschal mystery.

This relates with the "evangelical detachment" that all Christians are called to live. The people, situations, and material objects in one's life are to be a means of transformation rather than ends in themselves.[71] The words of Jesus are especially poignant for the celibate priest: "And everyone who has given up houses or brothers or sisters or father or mother or children or lands for the sake of my name will inherit a hundred times more, and will inherit eternal life" (Mt 19:29). (Luke adds "wife" to the list.) This giving up or leaving also demands letting go of any anger, grudges, and resentment toward members of one's family of origin. The priest must be able to live in the present, not stuck in unfinished or even hurtful issues of his past.

In healthy human living a balance and interplay among the three processes of thinking (cognition), feeling (affection) and acting (behavior) is needed. Solitude provides the opportunity to bear feelings. It also provides time for reflection on our experience of feelings and behavior. Reflection allows us to ponder important questions: What do these feelings mean? What is the message they are trying to reveal to me? How can I integrate these sexual desires into my celibate identity? What is God's invitation to ongoing personal and spiritual growth beneath these feelings and desires? What concrete decisions can I make about the specific behaviors I choose and the ones I choose to renounce?

Wholesome solitude helps to facilitate the passage from loneliness to aloneness. Loneliness, the awareness and pain of separation from others, what we lack, and what is absent from us, is finally resolved by aloneness, which includes the awareness of union and the awareness of what we have. This passage only occurs when we embrace and confront the pain of loneliness so that we can arrive at the other side. In the experience of aloneness we can feel, savor, realize, and accept who we really are, who others are, and who God is.[72]

There are many ways to foster and sustain a capacity for wholesome solitude and welcome its fruit. These include blocks of silence each day, solitary walks, a "desert day" of solitude periodically, going to a hermitage for a few days, doing a thirty-day retreat, and taking a sabbatical. Priestly celibacy will thrive when one's healthy and holy living includes the necessary experience of solitude.

Questions for Reflection

1. Describe the place of solitude and silence in your life. Do you welcome the opportunity to be alone? Is it a positive time for you?
2. In what ways does solitude faciliate your acknowledging, identifying, and bearing of feelings?
3. Is any loss a "front burner" issue for you right now?
4. Has any loss been "paschalized" for you? If so, describe the process.

IV. Age-Appropriate Psychosexual Development

Towards Psychosexual Maturity

Priestly celibacy demands an age-appropriate psychosexual maturity in a priesthood candidate. He should "give evidence of mature psychological and psychosexual development."[73]   A seminarian must know where he is in the schema of his psychosexual maturity and he must be intent on engaging in the life-long process of development. The first conversation between God and humans in the Bible begins with God's question: "Where are you?" (Gen 3:9) As with so many of the questions that God and Jesus ask in the Bible, this one engages the hearer/reader. It is a question that can apply to the grounding reality of our psychosexual maturity. It evokes the necessary starting point in formation for a life-long commitment to priestly celibacy. Where are you in the grounding reality of your sexuality? What is your sexual story? How do you feel about your sexual desires and fantasies? Are you at peace and do you feel emotionally alive without genital sex and a romantic relationship? Given your grounding reality, what do you sense as God's invitation for growth in terms of integration and freedom?

Contemporary understanding of the human person no longer speaks of maturity as an event that takes place in our early adult years. Rather, we speak of human maturation in terms of life stages, life cycles, and life tasks. Researchers have studied the stages of cognitive, social, psychological, moral, and faith development. Maturation is an ongoing process involving all aspects of what it means to be human.

This understanding of ongoing maturation has also begun to influence the way we understand our sexuality and our capacity to enter into and sustain human relationships. This developmental reality is reflected in a Vatican document concerning sexual ethics:

> According to contemporary scientific research, the human person is so profoundly affected by sexuality that it must be considered as one of the factors which give to each individual's life the principle traits that distinguish it. In fact it is from sex that the human person receives the characteristics which, on the biological, psychological and spiritual levels, make that person a man or a woman, and thereby largely condition his or her progress towards maturity and insertion into society.[74]

Six Dimensions of Psychosexual Development

Psychosexual development refers to the dynamic interplay of experiences, circumstances, phases, tasks, awarenesses, and decisions that lead us toward mature and loving relationships. Healthy psychosexual development includes the following six dimensions:

Physical: The genetic, biological hormonal factors that influence our sexual response from the first moments of conception and throughout the seasons of our lives.

Cognitive: Accurate and adequate sexual knowledge; the positive perception of our bodies; beliefs that reverence self and others.

Emotional: Being "at home" with our body; being aware of and comfortable with our sexual feelings; having healthy feelings toward others.

Social: Relating to others in unself-conscious ways; having the capacity for self-disclosure; being able to sustain friendship and intimacy.

Moral: Valuing the attitudes and actions that are necessary for ongoing sexual integration; expressions of our sexuality that are faithful, healthy, and other-enriching; behaviors that are congruent with our life commitments.

Spiritual: Affirming the presence of God and the sacred in our sexual feelings and expressions; coming to recognize that sexuality and spirituality are not enemies, but friends.[75]

When any of these dimensions are absent or limited, or if they develop in unhealthy ways, our journey toward sexual health and integration will be hindered, slowed down, or halted. Healthy human and sexual development also possess four qualities or "marks of health": emerging self-awareness, responsible freedom, developing creativity, and deepening capacity for intimacy.[76]

A definite harmony exists between the wholeness of life implied in these six dimensions and four qualities and the holiness of life to which all Christians are called. This connection is exemplified in the Latin word *salus*, which means both salvation and health, holiness and wholeness. These qualities and dimensions provide a framework for self-assessment. How do I experience the physical, cognitive, emotional, social, moral, and spiritual dimensions of my psychosexual development? Which ones are more developed? Which ones need further understanding, maturity, and integration? Using the four marks of health (self-awareness, responsible freedom, developing creativity, capacity for intimacy), how would I assess my own human and sexual development? What does this reflection suggest about where I am and how God is calling me to grow in wholeness and holiness?

Seminarians today come with a variety of growth issues in these six dimensions of psychosexual development and four marks of health. For some it is a lack of connection or integration among the various dimensions; their lives are fragmented or compartmentalized. For example, a student may exhibit a splitting between his sexuality and his spirituality. "Chuck" in the second vignette gives indications of this dualistic approach. Externally he maintains his devotional practices and searches for "orthodoxy." Internally he has many unresolved sexual issues indicated by his pattern of masturbation and vindictive behavior. Some students operate in an early stage of moral development. They blindly obey external laws about sexuality without internally appropriating the meaning and values behind the laws.

Emotional maturity is a challenge for many, usually due to a pattern of denial of feelings or a traumatic relationship in childhood. Their affective needs are often dismissed and their capacity for emotional warmth, tenderness, and compassion is limited. "This element [emotional maturity] is one of the major contributory processes in personality integration, in the unfolding of emotional and sexual relationships, finding responsible fulfillment in work or a profession, and in cultivating friendly social contacts."[77] This is a growth area for "Fritz" in the second vignette as he deals with the layers of intense emotions he felt in the encounter with the fourteen-year- old boy.

Patricia Livingston has designed a helpful continuum of human sexuality based on three areas: primary sexuality, genital sexuality, and affective sexuality. These are developed by William Kraft in his book *Sexual Dimensions of the Celibate Life* (see bibliography). Primary sexuality includes one's feelings about one's body and oneself as a man or a woman. Genital sexuality includes sexual stirrings, urges, desires, and physical reactions. Affective sexuality includes one's ability to feel close to people and express closeness, as well as to have a sense of boundaries in touch. A person may be non-assertive, assertive, or aggressive in his or her sexuality in these three areas.

Livingston's continuum of human sexuality and a set of corresponding reflection questions can be useful tools as a seminarian strives to locate himself in the grounding reality of his sexual identity. (See pages 69-71 for a diagram of the continuum and questions.) It can be used in his own self-reflection and in conversations with his spiritual director and other trusted mentors. This can lead to significant engagement with the primal question of our creating God: "Where are you?"

Sexual Integration

Psychosexual maturity entails the integration of one's sexual feelings and sexual identity. One's sexual identity is comprised of three dimensions: gender identity, sexual orientation, and sexual intention. Gender identity is the first aspect of sexual identity to form. A child develops a sense of being a boy or girl by the middle or end of the third year of life, probably based upon an inconspicuous, repetitive, labelling process underway since birth. The child is taught his or her gender and is subtly steered into a masculine or feminine direction. It is possible for a man to be genuinely masculine gender-identity deficient. This may be the case for a transsexual (a "woman in a man's body") and a transvestite (wearing women's clothing).

The second dimension of sexual identity is sexual orientation. Adult subjective orientation refers to the gender of persons or mental images of persons that attract and provoke sexual arousal. Adults are considered heteroerotic, homoerotic, or bierotic, depending on whether the great majority of images, fantasies, and attractions associated with sexual arousal concern members of the opposite gender, same gender, or both genders.

Sexual intention—what a person actually wants to do with a sexual partner— constitutes the third dimension of sexual identity. Conventional sexual intentions include kissing, caressing, and genital union, which are mutually pleasurable to consenting adults. Unconventional sexual intentions include sadism, masochism, exhibitionism, voyeurism, rape, and pedophilia. Erotic intention refers to the intrapsychic fantasy aspects. Behavioral intention refers to what would actually be acted out.[78]

This third dimension of sexual identity (sexual intention) is as important as the first (gender identity) and second (sexual orientation). Conventional erotic and behavioral sexual intentions reveal a person's health in seeking peaceable mutuality and tenderness. Unconventional sexual intentions reveal raw or disguised aggression toward self or other persons. Sexual intentions are manifested in one's attractions, fantasies, dreams, and (partner behavior for those who are sexually active). Obviously, severe unconventional intentions ought to raise red flags in a priesthood candidate and those who counsel him.[79]

Dr. John Money has coined the term "lovemap" as another way of speaking about sexual intention. A lovemap is a developmental representation or template in the mind and is dependent on input through the senses. It depicts a person's idealized lover and what, as a pair, they do together in the idealized, romantic, erotic, and sexualized relationship. A lovemap exists first in the mental imagery of dreams and fantasies, and then might be translated into action with a partner.[80]

Sexual integration for a priesthood candidate means awareness and honesty about his gender identity, sexual orientation, and sexual intentions. He must embrace and accept them *as they really are*, not as he wishes they might be. For many seminarians this means acknowledging a homosexual orientation, some homosexual attractions, or homophobia.

A decisive question for all seminarians—heterosexual, homosexual or bisexual—is whether they can make a lifelong commitment to celibate chastity and experience this lifestyle in a healthy and life-giving manner. Someone like "Arnie" in the third vignette obviously needs exploration of his ability to make a commitment to celibate chastity. He will also benefit from examining the issues beneath his anger towards the Church and his lack of total honesty about his behavior in his admissions interview.

A person is either egosyntonic or egodystonic in his sexual identity. The former state is one of being accepting, comfortable, and at peace with his sexual identity. The latter state is one of being uncomfortable and unaccepting of his sexual identity. This intrapsychic issue is a key distinction. Each seminarian must work at resolving any internal conflicts, guilt, shame, anxiety, or dissatisfaction concerning his sexual identity. He must arrive at a place of sexual maturity and integration so that he can spend his life in sacrificial service to the people of God rather than be fearful, preoccupied, or turned within himself. Persons who are egodystonic should not make a commitment to celibacy or marriage.

The Multi-Dimensional Nature of Homosexuality

Homosexuality is complex and multi-dimensional. A seminarian quickly announcing "I am gay" or a mentor saying "He must be a homosexual" are not helpful ways of dealing with sexual identity. "It makes more sense to ask about specific aspects of same-gender behavior, practice, and feelings during specific periods of an individual's life rather than a single yes-or-no question about whether a person is homosexual."[81] For descriptive purposes, there are three identifiable dimensions of homosexuality: same-gender sexual behavior, same-gender desire and sexual attraction as internal psychological states, and self-identity as a homosexual person. Sometimes this third dimension is divided into two components: one's inner (private) perceived sense of identity, and one's social role or public declaration of being homosexual.[82] Homosexuality is manifested in a complex interrelationship among these cognitive, affective, and behavioral dimensions of being human.

Erotic fantasies, sexual activity with others (or sexual intention), sense of identity, and social role may be congruent or incongruent in a given individual. For instance, a man may fantasize about sex with men, engage exclusively in homoerotic acts or have homosexual intentions, feel that his inner identity is homosexual, and be publicly known as gay. Or an individual may have sexual fantasies predominately about males, engage in sexual activity with both men and women or have bisexual intentions, feel that his inner identity is homosexual, but may live publicly (either single or married) as a heterosexual. Another man may identify himself as heterosexual, have heterosexual intentions, and have predominantly heterosexual fantasies and periodic homosexual desires. Adopting a heterosexual social role even if one has predominantly homosexual fantasies and a sense of homosexual identity is understandably common in homophobic social settings.[83]

"It is important to state here that a person who is homosexual and has not made this self-awareness known to others (has not "come out") can surely be as honest, integral and self-possessed (ego-syntonic) as a gay or lesbian person."[84] (The terms "gay" and "lesbian" refer to the public declaration of one's sexual orientation.) It is possible to live a life of honesty and integrity without being recognized as a homosexually- oriented person in the public world. At the same time, it would be very difficult for a person to feel genuinely close to at least a small number of people without them being aware of his sexual orientation. Personal support is critical.

Gerald Coleman's text, *Homosexuality: Catholic Teaching and Pastoral Practice*

(1995), is very helpful in shedding light on this complex issue. He carefully researches this topic from the perspectives of psychology, Scripture, Catholic morality, and pastoral practice. I recommend it to anyone who desires to grow in greater understanding of this aspect of the human experience.

Concerns About Masturbation

For a fair number of men concerns about masturbation are evident in their psychosexual development. Richard Sipe reports that masturbation is the most common and frequently used sexual behavior of celibates.[85] The Chicago Study findings show that 80% of men who have graduate degrees reported masturbating in the past year.[86] Sipe has a chapter titled "The Masturbations" (plural).[87] He describes different scenarios that involve varying degrees of pathology, personal maturity, moral development, and spiritual development.

Compulsive masturbation or autoeroticism, that is, masturbating several times a day, is clinically described as nonparaphilic compulsive sexual behavior. Masturbation becomes part of an obsessive-compulsive drive that is driven by anxiety-reduction mechanisms rather than by sexual desire. The obsessive thought and compulsive behaviors reduce anxiety and distress, but they also create a self-perpetuating cycle.[88] It is possible for this sexual addiction or compulsion to be so self-preoccupying in a person's life that his ability for self-sacrificing love and service is severely limited. Then the question arises as to whether he is a viable candidate for a life-time commitment to celibate chastity and ordained priesthood.

Occasional masturbation is often a developmental issue. It "results in the achievement of sexual gratification with no interest in satisfying the needs of another person. It belongs initially to the narcissistic phase of libidinal development. When continued as a major or predominant form of sexual activity, it can be classified as a narcissistic perversion or form of self-love."[89]

Masturbation for an adult points to the unfinished nature of a person's sexual and spiritual integration as a human being. In counseling people it is important to focus not so much on the action but on what the action is signifying and revealing. Masturbation is symptomatic of intrapersonal and interpersonal conflicts like boredom, frustration, poor self-image, inadequate relationships, conflict with people, pressure, and lack of peace about sexual fulfillment. It expresses some internal psychological state that needs attention. So it is helpful to look for general lifestyle and behavior patterns in a person who struggles with masturbation.

Both psychologists and theologians have come to emphasize that the fantasies that accompany masturbation are important and useful indicators of what masturbation means, first humanly and then morally.[90] They give a clue to one's sexual intentions. They may reveal sadistic, masochistic, incestuous, pedophilic, or self-glorifying thoughts. These fantasies may give rise to more guilt than the masturbatory behavior itself.

Vincent Genovesi provides a very helpful discussion of the psychological and human meanings of masturbation, moral evaluations, and pastoral advice in his text, *In Pursuit of Love:Catholic Morality and Human Sexuality*.[91] The *Catechism* offers some sound advice regarding moral culpability. "To form an equitable judgment about the subjects' moral responsibility and to guide pastoral action, one must take into account the affective immaturity, force of acquired habit, conditions of anxiety, or other psychological or social factors that lessen or even extenuate moral culpability."[92] The goal for persons who struggle with masturbation is to progress toward freedom that is reflective of dealing with intrapersonal and interpersonal developmental issues and that approaches the Church's vision of "perfect and perpetual continence."[93]

Adulthood is Developmental

Some people are stuck at an adolescent or preadolescent phase of psychosexual development. This is the "chum period,"[94] prior to 11 years of age when boys prefer association with their own sex. They avoid girls and hold them in disdain, often as a guise for fear of women and as a protection for themselves and their own unsolidified sexual identity. Externally they rigidly deny sex while internally they secretly explore it. Control, avoidance, and defensiveness are significant issues. For their own health and for the sake of the Church, they ought to mature beyond this stage.

Adulthood itself is developmental. Early adulthood is a time of relational exploration and experimentation during which cultural myths and stereotypes about sexuality, relationships, and intimacy are challenged, questioned, and sometimes shattered. The focus shifts from quantity of relationships to quality of relationships. There also is a shift from external reference for personal validation to an internal reference for authority and authenticity. One's decisions and behaviors are no longer determined by what others think, but come from one's inner sense of what is valuable and less valuable, what is loving and unloving, what is right and wrong. The mid-life passage or transition entails a process of interiorization and appreciation for one's essential aloneness. "Adult transitions are relational transitions,"[95] with the task of re-evaluating and re-ordering one's relationships with self, God, and others.

Intimacy, sexuality, and celibacy can be identified as products or as processes. Neither approach embraces the whole reality; each needs the other for balance. People need to have a sense of what sexuality is (product) so that they can identify and grow into it through their lived experiences of ever-changing self-understanding (process). Too much of an emphasis on product leads to stagnation and rigidity, whereas too much emphasis on process leads to chaotic anarchy.[96] In his article, "Taking a Sexual History,"[97] Gerald Coleman provides a helpful discussion of the importance of understanding how a candidate experiences, manages, and integrates his sexual feelings, especially in light of his hope to make a permanent commitment to celibate chasity. He has a useful set of reflection questions that address various areas of concern as one engages in a process of sexual integration. These areas of concern include an absence of sexual awareness, a spiritualization of sexuality, excessive scruples or moralizing around sexuality, compulsive sexual behavior, and denial of sexual feelings.

Priestly celibacy demands psychosexual maturity in the lives of the men who want to make a life-long commitment to this way of loving and serving in the Church. It is critical that seminarians take full advantage of the seminary formation program and any other beneficial resources to facilitate their ongoing development. We now turn to another necessary element in celibacy formation—the capacity for intimacy in human friendships, the complement of the capacity for solitude.

Questions for Reflection

1. How would you respond to the scriptural question "Where are you?" concerning your psychosexual development?
2. How are you being called to further sexual integration and freedom?
3. How do you experience the six dimensions of healthy psychosexual development? Are any of them underdeveloped? Do you experience any splitting?
4. What questions remain for you in your psychosexual development and in your sexual integration?

V. Capacity for Intimacy in Human Friendships

Two Kinds of Intimacy

A priest experiences two kinds of intimacy: ministerial intimacy and the intimacy of close friendships. As an ordained minister he is involved in people's lives in some of their most sacred, personal, and intimate moments. He is present to them in times of great joy and great crisis from the womb to the tomb. He listens to their story in pastoral counseling and as they confess their sins. These are experiences of ministerial intimacy for the priest, but they are one-sided. There is no mutuality, since the priest does not share with them his troubles or pain. A priest becomes entrapped in either loneliness or boundary violations if he relies on ministerial intimacy as his only experience of drawing close to people. The healthy priest needs the second kind of intimacy, that of sustaining friendships where he experiences closeness and personal support.

A celibate person is a sexual person with real intimacy needs that must be met in appropriate and fulfilling ways. This can happen only when a person has developed the affective and relational side of what it means to be a sexual being as well as the biological and physiological side. The tender and compassionate person is one who has reached sexual integration and maturity. "It is the goal of celibate love to socialize and universalize one's affectivity in the direction of compassion, which is the supreme sign of an integrated sexual life."[98]

It is not possible for human beings to draw close to each other in chaste intimacy unless they experience authentic self-intimacy. This entails a growing tolerance and comfortableness with who we are—a mix of both strengths and weaknesses—exhibited in the ability to be alone in healthy solitude. The unhealthy extremes are hiding in isolation, and being afraid of ever being alone. Mature self-intimacy entails taking moments in a day and a full day or so periodically to withdraw for self-reflection; awareness of inner movements leads to acceptance of them, which in turn leads to action based on the choices that are available.

Erikson describes intimacy as "the capacity to commit oneself to concrete affiliations and partnerships and to develop the ethical strength to abide by such commitments, even though they may call for significant sacrifice and compromise."[99] Intimacy with others is the experience of connectedness, a simultaneous fusing and counterpointing. There is an interplay between two opposing dynamics: the pull of self-disclosure and empathy, and the pull of caution and selectivity in what is shared with whom. Authentic intimacy with others necessitates self-disclosure, vulnerability, and mutuality. Intimacy is the feeling of closeness established when two people share deep and important things about themselves with each other, including their weaknesses, fears, and struggles.

Intimacy Needs

Keith Clark provides a helpful approach to sexuality and intimacy in the celibate context. He describes three levels of the human experience of being sexual: as experienced in biological urges, bio-psychological drives, and personal-spiritual needs. On the level of biological urges men experience the physical sexual responses of arousal, erections, and nocturnal emissions. On the second level of bio-psychological drives they experience the emotional romantic responses of attraction, infatuation, and falling in love. Certain types of people have a sexual significance for each person on an emotional or romantic level. On the level of personal-spiritual needs they experience a deep need for intimacy in sharing hopes and fears, successes and failures. Sexual fulfillment is found in the attainment of inter-personal intimacy needs and not in the gratification of biological urges or romantic drives alone.[100]

In each level Clark distinguishes between *responses* and *pursuits*. We all naturally experience genital responses, romantic responses, and intimacy responses. We have a choice of consciously pursuing these responses, or simply being aware of them, accepting them, and letting them be. Some behaviors are healthy and appropriate for the chaste celibate person; others are not. For example, we may impulsively choose to sexually act out in genital involvement with another person or in masturbation. We may choose to deny the sexual feelings or try to get rid of them. Or we may choose to let ourselves experience the physical and romantic responses without pursuing them, without doing something about them; they came and they will go. This last choice is the chaste option for the celibate person. This approach exhibits responsibility and integrity in being a sexual celibate.

It is the deep level of need for human intimacy, Clark asserts, that must be pursued to bring about sexual integration and sexual fulfillment. We may get a clue about the value of intimacy when we are away from our support network of friends and family. It is then that our sexual urges may get stronger because we are away from those who are close to us, those who help us to meet our intimacy needs.

Sensuousness, play, and pleasure are important in inter-personal intimacy and psychosexual growth. Games, hobbies, nature, and the arts give us a sense of enjoyment and help us to experience beauty. In this way sexual energy can be diffused throughout the entire body-person and not remain largely genital in nature or cause a person to appear rather wooden. A regular pattern of physical exercise honors and supports this holistic and integrative sense of the human person.

Barriers to Intimacy

True human intimacy is a way of being close to other people that avoids the extremes of over-involvement and under-involvement in their lives. This balanced way of relating intimately is learned from mentors, from experience, and from reflecting on one's experience. For persons who struggle with establishing and maintaining appropriately close relationships, it is possible to uncover barriers to intimacy in one's attitudes or subconscious. Sean Sammon provides a helpful discussion of these barriers in his book, *An Undivided Heart*.[101] In this section I will be closely following his contributions.

Distortions in the way a person thinks are barriers that limit a person's ability to enhance the possibility of intimacy in his or her life. Poor self-image, low self-esteem, equating intimacy with genitality, and expecting to be perfect are a few of these cognitive distortions.

Another barrier, Sammon asserts, is fear of self-disclosure. There may be a reluctance to express strong positive emotions like affection and gratitude, or other emotions like hurt and fear. It is also possible to be living out of the myth that if I tell anyone something important about myself, that person will have power over me.

Fears of dependence (more often in men) or abandonment (more often in women) cause difficulty in establishing intimacy. Men may pull back and may be threatened in situations in which they must be dependent on others, complaining about being smothered. A male friend may seem inaccessible to a woman; she may feel frustrated that the relationship isn't developing more deeply.

Misuse of listening skills can be a barrier. This can happen if we are too clinical or too therapeutic in our approach to someone—wanting to know all the details but in a very one-sided exchange. It can also happen if our only "intimate" conversations are with a counselor, spiritual director, or confessor. Mutuality is key in inter-personal intimacy.

Homophobia impedes intimacy. This irrational fear of homosexuality, fear of persons who are gay or lesbian, or fear of our own attractions to persons of our gender can lead to hostility and anger. Myths, fears, and stereotypes abound in this arena.

A final barrier to intimacy, Sammon points out, is dysfunctional background related to family of origin issues. Our list might include the following: denial, avoidance of issues, fear of conflict, inability to express anger appropriately, the silent treatment, rigidity, and isolation. Members of a troubled family deny feelings and facts about behavior, fail to talk about what is going on, lack trust, and isolate themselves from one another and from those outside the group.

These are all impediments to authentic inter-personal intimacy and can be read as danger signs. At times they are pointed out to a person by classmates, associates, teachers, counselors, and spiritual directors. These people act as a kind of mirror for us, reflecting back to us the reality that they see and we do not see. It is a great gift, a great opportunity that can lead eventually to greater interior freedom and whole-some friendships.

Establishing Appropriate Friendships

Seminarians and priests need close friendships with a variety of people—men and women, young and old, ordained, religious, and lay. If a man purposefully restricts his friendships to one category, it is indicative of some underlying attitude or prejudice that needs purification. Candidates for the priesthood need an affective maturity that is "capable of esteem and respect in interpersonal relationships with men and women."[102] In the Gospels Jesus is portrayed as having close relationships with men and women. "Now Jesus loved Martha and her sister and Lazarus" (Jn 11:5). "Accompanying him were the Twelve and some women who had been cured of evil spirits and infirmities, Mary, called Magdalene, from whom seven demons had gone out, Joanna, the wife of Herod's steward Chuza, Susanna, and many others who provided for them out of their resources" (Lk 8:1-3).

The love that a priest is to experience in these friendships is inclusive, personal, and individual. It is not a "love" that is possessive, pre-occupying, exclusive, or secretive. Appropriate levels of physical and emotional intimacy need to be established in friendships. If a particular friendship becomes characteristic of romantic or spousal love, deep emotional involvement, or a pre-marital courtship, then a serious assessment is necessary. There is obviously a danger in fostering friendships with persons who are erotically attractive to us—men or women, depending on our sexual orientation. These are times to keep our goal and commitment in clear sight. A crucial question to ask is what direction is this relationship headed? Is it moving toward an exclusive spousal relationship?

Many people struggling with the issue of celibate love will ask: "How far can I go?" Coombs and Nemeck assert that this is an incorrect question that reflects a legalistic or static mind-set and focusses on physical acts. This question, they suggest, implies another: "How far can I gratify my appetites, my desires, my self?" There is another approach that exercises personal responsibility and respects the sense of vocation; it appreciates human attitudes and actions in light of their effects on the loved one and on the dynamics of the relationship. The critical question to ask is: "How much interaction is necessary in the celibate love relationship to attain an optimum of spirit and yet preserve its celibate quality?" The word "optimum" highlights a qualitative mode rather than a quantitative one. The two persons in the celibate love relationship are called not to a mediocre or compromising affection, but to the most qualitative sense of *agape* possible. Instead of cutting off the relationship, they struggle to let their love become all that God desires it to be.[103]

A Charism of Relationship

Celibacy is a charism of relationship for the Church.[104] With his vision on the building up of the Body of Christ and the proclamation of the Gospel, the celibate priest facilitates the sense of *communio* that all members of the Church are to have with each other in Christ. The priest spends his life mirroring the life of the Trinity: the inner life of *communio*, life-giving and love-giving generativity, and an outward sense of mission. "Exercising, within the limits of the authority which is theirs, the office of Christ, the Shepherd and Head, [priests] assemble the family of God as brothers and sisters animated by the spirit of unity, and through Christ in the Spirit that leads them to God the Father."[105]

The charism of celibacy is a way of loving others for life. It is a challenge, not because it is a sacrifice of our humanity, our sexuality, and our masculinity, but because it will demand living our humanity, sexuality, and masculinity to the fullest. In order to succeed (to be faithful and to be happy) the celibate priest must know the first love—God's love for him and for all people; he must experience celibate chastity as sexually fulfilling; and he must experience love in his personal and pastoral relationships.

There is a vital connection between the experience of human friendships and the experience of contemplative prayer addressed in the second section of this essay. Ernest Larkin, a renowned Carmelite scholar, examines this connection as it is treated in the writings of St. Teresa of Avila. She teaches us the importance of spiritual love in human friendships and that this love has its source in God's love. "The decisive consideration for spiritual love is its grounding. It originates in the experience of God's love freely received and deeply experienced in contemplation. The spiritual quality of all graced love for others, imperfect as well as perfect, has its source in God's prior, gracious love."[106] This truth is found in the Johannine literature: "In this is love: not that we have loved God, but that he loved us and sent his Son as expiation for our sins. Beloved, if God so loved us, we also must love one another" (I Jn 4:10-11).

The perfect form of this spiritual love is nurtured in contemplation. This is how Teresa describes it:

> Now it seems to me that those whom God brings to a certain clear knowledge love very differently than do those who have not reached it. This clear knowledge is about the nature of the world, that there is another world, about the difference between the one and the other, that the one is eternal and the other a dream; or about the nature of loving the Creator and loving the creature (and this is seen through experience, which is entirely different from merely thinking about it or believing it).[107]

In both prayer and human love attention is given to the primacy of the indwelling presence of God. "In prayer the goal is to allow the indwelling Presence to transform the person; in human love the objective is to let the divine love which has been received find expression in symbolic ways."[108] This way of living calls for cooperation with God's initiating love and a determined decision to respond in loving communion with others.

The spiritual love in human relationships, as Teresa teaches, is not the popular therapeutic notion of human love, nor is it a stoic or over-spiritualized love. This genuine spiritual love is found in a fully mature, whole, and integrated relationship. It is a matter of the heart and as such involves the whole person.[109]

It will seem to you that such persons [who love with spiritual love] do not love anyone but God. I say, yes, they do love, with a greater and genuine love, and with passion and with a more beneficial love; in short it is love. And these souls are more inclined to give than to receive.[110]

The experience of spiritual love and intimacy in human relationships are essential in the lives of seminarians and priests. It takes energy and a profound reverence to establish and foster these sustaining friendships. (See the work sheet on page 72 titled "Circles of Relationships in a Priest's Life" and the one titled "Reflecting on Relational Development" on page 73 for exercises that focus on this topic.) This leads us to the next guiding element in formation for priestly celibacy—experiencing the support of the faith community.

Questions for Reflection
1. How would you describe your intimacy needs?
2. What is attractive to you about intimacy in friendships? What is scary?
3. What barriers to intimacy do you see in yourself? What barriers do other people see in you?
4. "Celibacy is a charism of relationship in the Church." How do you envision this to be the case for you?

VI. Experience of Community Support

Celibate chastity is a gift to the Church, the entire body of the faithful. As a gift of the Spirit of God to the Christian community, it can also be the community's corporate gift to society, through which we make personally present our belief in the transcendent, inclusive, universal, and non-violent dimensions of human relationships. The call to celibacy as a viable and life-giving way of living the Christian journey must be part of and for the good of the entire community, including the secular community.[111]

The Church has an obligation to foster an environment of respect for the gift of celibacy and it has an obligation to support particular persons who espouse celibacy as a way of life. Seminarians and priests are right to expect assistance and encouragement in the initial and ongoing formation for celibate chastity. Because the gift of celibacy is not purely a private matter but a community sign affecting the entire community, seminarians and priests should also expect to be accountable to the community for their expression of it.

The parish where a seminarian experiences his pastoral formation provides a local opportunity for him to experience this support and accountability. In the heterogeneous community of a support group comprised of men and women with varied life experiences, educational and occupational backgrounds, and religious values, the candidate can experience a microcosm of the parish and of the Church itself. This small formative group provides opportunities for human interaction and engagement with the whole spectrum of human relationships in their creative variety. "The true life of God is revealed as one's false ego-structures are dismantled, as one's fear and defensiveness are exorcised, and as one is allowed to stand and be, transparent and frail, in need of and being needed by the community."[112]

Faithful Models

The seminarian's most immediate inspiration and instruction for celibate chastity comes from the modeling of other faithful celibates. The seminary provides the candidate with the presence of a celibate community, including both professed celibates on the faculty and fellow seminarians. Here he should be able to find models and companions on the journey.[113] It is important to spend quality time with persons who share the same values and ideals.

Priests have a special responsibility to be viable witnesses of priestly celibacy for seminarians. It is important for a seminarian to know some priests who speak directly about their experience of priestly celibacy: this is my story; this is how my experience of celibate chastity has developed; these have been my struggles; this is how it makes sense to me; this is how I feel fulfilled and happy as a celibate priest. This kind of practical and anecdotal sharing is key. Seminarians need eldering and mentoring on this journey of formation. They need wise and seasoned priests to guide and accompany them.

The example of Christian chastity from religiously committed lay students and faculty is also formative. Each person remaining faithful to his or her chosen lifestyle sets an example for the seminarian and encourages him to reflect on his own experience. Celibacy and chastity are not merely concepts but are realities lived by particular persons. Conversation and encouragement among other believers concerning the virtue of chastity is beneficial in the formation process.

When someone in the seminary violates the common expectations around celibate chastity, whether this be a faculty member who sexually exploits a student or sexually harasses a colleague, a student flaunting a girlfriend, two seminarians becoming excessively preoccupied with one another, or someone impulsively terminating his participation in the program, people may feel angry or disillusioned. Questions are raised about integrity and faithfulness that need to be addressed and processed.

The homosocial environment of the seminary has its limiting characteristics because of the high percentage of males around the same age. But close contact with other males can also be very helpful in the formation process. A man's anxieties about masculinity and his prejudices against women become exposed in a way that he does not anticipate. These reactions can then be dealt with in formation advising, spiritual direction, and counseling. This heavy male context can push a seminarian to face his homophobia or, especially in the case of a homosexual candidate, to work through his sexual attractions toward male friends. In these real-life relationships the seminarian is clarifying his suitability for celibacy and preparing for his interactions with other priests.[114]

Sacramental Brotherhood

The Vatican II documents are clear that a priest's sacramental relationship with his bishop and fellow priests is part of his identity. "In virtue of their sacred ordination and of their common mission, all priests are united together by bonds of intimate brotherhood. This should manifest itself in mutual help, spiritual or temporal, pastoral or personal, spontaneously and freely given in reunions and togetherness in life, work and charity."[115] "All priests, who are constituted in the order of priesthood by the sacrament of order, are bound together by an intimate sacramental brotherhood; but in a special way they form one priestly body in the diocese to which they are attached under their own bishop. . . Each is joined to the rest of the members of this priestly body by special ties of apostolic charity, of ministry and of fellowship."[116]

In light of this vision and the necessity of experiencing community support, there are at least three implications for seminarians during their time of formation, a time that ought to be a kind of apprenticeship for this intimate sacramental brotherhood. First, seminarians ought to experience a brotherhood among themselves that is marked by care, respect, encouragement, and fellowship. Even their living together on the same floor with other seminarians prepares them for the day when they will need to cooperate with other priests who happen to be close to them in the same deanery. Factions and cliques are deformative to this vision of the Church.

Second, during their time of formation seminarians should make every effort to be part of groups of seminarians and groups of seminarians and priests that meet regularly. These gatherings can foster a spirit of *communio* by sharing meals, leisure activities, prayer, and personal struggles and successes. These groups will prepare the seminarian for the day when he will be part of a priest support group. No one knows the joys and challenges of a priest more than another priest.

Third, it is important for a seminarian to be in contact with priests from his diocese during his years of formation, especially if the seminary is in a diocese other than his home diocese. He is being trained to serve in his home diocese. Fostering relationships with priests in his diocese will facilitate a connection with his brother priests that will continue when he begins his ministry with them. Summers and vacations may prove to be opportune times to connect with priests.

"The entire training program [including celibacy formation] is to be so organized that, with its atmosphere of piety, recollection and mutual support, it becomes a kind of initiation to the students' future lives as priests."[117] Seminarians need the support and encouragement of the community as they prepare for life-long priestly celibacy.

This support must continue after ordination. In order to stir into flame the gift of God, priests need the particular support of *pareneisis* that focuses specifically on priestly celibacy in the context of spirituality in diocesan priesthood. *Pareneisis* is exhortation, consolation, and confirmation that is patterned after the encouragement that Paul offers to the presbyters of Ephesus in the discourse of Miletus (Acts 20:18-38). The spirit of this reanimation is to strengthen, confirm, and reinforce the presbyters in their original commitment.[118] Retreats, workshops, and group discussions especially during the first years after ordination will help to support the careful attention given to this charism in the seminary program.

Questions for Reflection

1. Who are faithful models of priestly celibacy for you? Who are models of the virtue of chastity? What have they taught you? How have they influenced you?
2. Where do you find your greatest support for living a life of celibate chastity?
3. In what ways do you feel connected with the "intimate brotherhood" of priests in your diocese?

VII. Accountability to Others

Ongoing Accountability

The final guiding element in formation for priestly celibacy is honesty in one's accountability to others. As a public commitment and as a gift for the entire Church, the practice of celibate chastity by particular persons demands honest appraisal and accountability. One of the dangers of the lifestyle of diocesan priesthood is that it is possible for a priest to be a "lone ranger," devoid of close friends, a support group, competent spiritual direction, and appropriate mentoring or supervision. It is possible to hide in isolation or in workaholic practice. None of these dangerous lifestyles embody the vision of chastity that entails right relationships with God, self, and others.

Ongoing accountability, which must be fostered in the seminary, serves two purposes. First, it shatters the illusion that "my sexuality is only between me and God" or "between me and my confessor." It encourages examination of ideas or assumptions that might need to be modified or brought into the light of community in order to purify any misogynous or other unhealthy tendencies that may be present in a person. Second, accountability serves to draw the person's consciousness to a new level of awareness of his place in and his ministry to the community that is comprised of both married and celibate people who have a stake in the ongoing mission of the Church. Accountability provides a challenge that will dramatically confront any egocentric or narcissistic tendencies.[119]

Honesty in accountability must be part of a larger process of identifying and forthrightly dealing with any unhealthy propensities that might lead to tragedy later on. "Those who are discovered to be unfit—either for physical, psychological or moral reasons—should be quickly removed from the path to priesthood. . . The life of the celibate priest, which engages the whole man so totally and so delicately, excludes in fact those of insufficient psycho-physical and moral balance."[120]

The Program of Priestly Formation is very clear about the need for candidates to give testimony of a sustained habit of celibate chastity and of mature psychological and psychosexual development. These considerations are to be thoroughly treated in the admission process and in the continuing evaluation of seminarians. The rector, formation advisor, pastoral supervisor, and faculty in general must be able to attest whether a candidate exhibits a positive understanding of and readiness for living a celibate life, relating with other people in a mature fashion. Benefit of the doubt must always be given in favor of the concern of the Church.[121]

Spiritual direction is a confidential relationship in which the seminarian must be as honest and transparent as possible. "Personal relationships, sexuality, celibate chastity, commitment, and interiorization are essential topics for spiritual direction. In this setting, seminarians should be encouraged to speak in detail about their own personal struggles and review their success and failure in living a chaste, celibate life."[122] Spiritual direction is a privileged means of guidance in the process of conversion of mind and heart and in priestly formation.

Another place of accontability is the parish setting with the opportunity for supervised ministry. Here the seminarian speaks with his supervisor about boundaries in pastoral relationships and about transference and countertransference issues. This process helps to foster respect and clarity in ministerial relationships and assists the student in attending to developmental and personal growth needs.

Boundaries in Pastoral Relationships

In recent years we have witnessed a growing sensitivity to the boundaries of the professional-client relationship, such as priest-parishioner, faculty-student, and seminarian (intern)-parishioner. This dimension of human conduct is intricately related to chastity. Boundary violations in these relationships can be defined in terms of content; for example, sexual abuse of a minor or a vulnerable adult, sexual exploitation of a person under one's pastoral care, and sexual harassment of a co-worker. They can also be defined in terms of the context of the professional-client relationship itself.

There are four characteristics of a boundary violation.[123] First, the professional and client switch places and the client is expected to be the caretaker. The professional manipulates the inside of the relationship to meet his or her own needs. Second, there is a double and clandestine agenda. Important information or behavior is secretly kept from the client. Third, the client is caught in a double bind, a conflict of interest. In speaking up the client risks losing help and risks being punished or rejected. Fourth, in every boundary violation there is the indulgence of personal privilege, a conflict between the professional's need and the client's vulnerability. This inappropriate coupling produces the opportunity for the professional to take advantage of the client.

Boundaries in relationships have texture. They can be placed on a continuum ranging from rigid to structured to flexible to fluid to chaotic. Ministerial boundaries that are too rigid or too fluid can prove problematic. It is helpful to think of boundaries in terms of time, place, and person in order to monitor their appropriateness. Meeting with a client late at night can be risky. Blurring of boundaries occurs when committee meetings take place in a priest's living room and when private conferences are held in bedrooms. Personal boundaries are unique to each individual. For example, it is important for us to consider the impact of touch on the recipient as well as our motivation for doing the touching. Hugging a grieving woman might be interpreted by the woman, because of some past traumatic experience, as a threat or as a sexual invitation.[124]

Needless to say, great care and honesty are needed in being reflective on one's professional and ministerial relationships.   An internal sense of personal limits and professional boundaries, and utilizing the services of supervision are essential in dealing with the live issues that surface in transference and countertransference. The sacredness of pastoral relationships and our faith in a professional's abilities must be held up as great values and as ways in which God can do healing works.

Clear Behavorial Expectations

A seminary must have a clearly written policy concerning behavioral expectations. Here is an example of such a statement of expectations at The Saint Paul Seminary.

> If it becomes known that a seminarian is engaging in physical genital activity while he is in the seminary, he will be asked to leave. Certain other behaviors are inconsistent with celibate chastity: engaging in flirtatious or seductive behavior, dating, visiting pornographic bookstores and movies, and visiting singles or "pick-up" bars. A student who engages in any of the above behaviors is subject to dismissal from the seminary.

> Participating in or advocating the homosexual subculture are also unacceptable. They make service to the whole Church difficult or impossible.

> Sexualized conversation is inconsistent with the development of celibate chastity and has no place in the seminary. Examples of such conversation are those that reduce persons to sexual objects, those that interpret the words of others in a sexual manner, and those that even implicitly involve the propositioning of others in the community.

> A broad range of friendships with men and women is necessary for the living of celibate chastity. Preoccupation with sexual orientation or restricting one's friendships solely on the basis of a person's sexual orientation manifests a narrowness and selectivity inappropriate for a candidate for the priesthood who is called to extend pastoral charity to all people.

> Sexual abuse, sexual exploitation, and sexual harassment are properly understood as psychologically pathological behaviors rather than as specific violations of celibate chastity. Such actions are illegal and against explicit University [of St. Thomas] directives. They will not be tolerated. The policy of the school regarding these behaviors is presented in the student handbook [of the University].

> In the development of celibate chastity, candidates for the priesthood owe one another respect, care, and help. Above all, this requires that students be witnesses of integrity in their own pursuit of celibate chastity. There also are

43

some very specific considerations when a student has concerns about the behavior of other students. Under no circumstances may a student report to a third student or group of students his concerns about the real or imagined sexual behavior or orientation of another student. A student who has legitimate concerns about the behavior of another student should express those concerns directly to the other student; if the concerns are serious, they should be reported directly to the rector of the seminary.[125]

Specific behavioral expectations such as those listed above give a clear picture of what is appropriate and provide a benchmark in calling people to honesty and accountability. As public ministers in the Church priests have a special responsibility to be models and teachers of chastity for married, celibate, and single persons alike. Formation begins in the early years of life and is intensified and focused in the seminary program.

A good rule of thumb in assessing one's level of honesty concerning a particular behavior is to ask oneself: "Am I willing to talk about this with another person?" Sexual secrets must be brought into the light of day, illumined by the light of Christ and the community of faith. Honesty in accountability to the Church through friends, formation faculty, and trusted guides are essential in the life of celibate chastity.

In the end we are all also accountable to God. "So then each of us shall give an account of himself to God" (Rom 14:12). St. Paul gives an exhortation to holiness in sexual conduct. Some Bibles use "Charity and Chastity" as a heading for this section of this early Christian instruction:

> Finally, brothers and sisters, we ask and urge you in the Lord Jesus that, as you learned from us how you ought to live and to please God (as, in fact, you are doing), you should do so more and more. For you know what instructions we gave you through the Lord Jesus. For this is the will of God, your sanctification: that you abstain from fornication; that each one of you know how to control your own body in holiness and honor, not with lustful passion, like the Gentiles who do not know God; that no one wrong or exploit a brother or sister in this matter, because the Lord is an avenger in all these things, just as we have already told you beforehand and solemnly warned you. For God did not call us to impurity but to holiness. Therefore whoever rejects this rejects not human authority but God, who also gives his Holy Spirit to you (I Thes 4:1-8, NRSV).

The Sacrament of Penance, personal prayer, spiritual direction, support groups, and honest feedback from other people become avenues to bring us face to face with the truth.

Questions for Reflection

1. To whom do you manifest the greatest accountability regarding celibate chastity? To whom do you need to be more accountable or more honest? Do you have any "sexual secrets?"

2. Describe your sense of boundaries in your friendships and pastoral relationships. What kind of feedback do you get from peers? from those in authority over you? from parishioners?

3. Are there any behavioral expectations that are a challenge for you? If so, do you know why? What resources are available that can assist you in dealing with your issues?

Summary: Seven Essential Guiding Elements

Students like Fritz, Chuck, and Arnie will benefit greatly in the process of discernment about and preparation for priestly celibacy in a program of celibacy formation that includes these seven essential guiding elements. First, celibacy must be understood and experienced in the whole context of spirituality in diocesan priesthood, embracing the values of prayer, simplicity of life, obedience, pastoral service, and celibate chastity. All of these values must be internalized and appropriated as meaningful and life-giving experiential realities. Priestly celibacy is rightly understood both as a charism in the Church and as a developmental process that needs to be fostered and assessed.

Second, priestly celibacy cannot be sustained without a pattern of contemplative prayer that is intent upon noticing the transforming and liberating presence of God in the Liturgy, in God's Word, and in the traces of the paschal mystery found in living the Christian life. A commitment to celibate chastity must be made out of a transcendental motivation, that is, a personal experience of being overwhelmed by the reign of God.

Third, priestly celibacy demands being comfortable with solitude. The experience of solitude provides a way of acknowledging, identifying, and bearing feelings of frustration, anxiety, sadness, and pressure. A celibate person must be able to grieve the losses of genital sexual activity, conjugal love, and natural fatherhood, all of which are renounced for the sake of the Kingdom of God.

Fourth, age-appropriate psychosexual maturity is foundational. Psychosexual maturity entails the integration of one's sexual identity, sexual feelings, and sexual orientation. A student must become comfortable with his sexual identity and must resolve any internal conflicts, guilt, shame, or anxiety about sexual issues so that he can give of himself in pastoral charity.

Fifth, a celibate person is a sexual person with real intimacy needs that must be met in appropriate and fulfilling friendships. This can only happen when a person has developed the affective and relational side of what it means to be a sexual being as well as the biological and psychological side. The experience of tenderness and closeness in friendships is essential in sustaining a life of celibate chastity.

Sixth, the seminarian's most immediate inspiration and instruction for celibate chastity comes from the modeling and support of other faithful celibates. It is necessary that he experience himself as part of the celibate community comprised of professed celibates and fellow seminarians who accompany him on the journey.

The seminarian must know and contribute to a spirit of reverence and respect for the gift of celibacy in the Church.

Seventh, as a public commitment and as a gift for the entire Church, the practice of celibate chastity by particular persons demands honest appraisal and accountability. Spiritual direction, pastoral supervision, faculty advising, and relationships with peers provide avenues for accountability. Unhealthy propensities and patterns in friendships and pastoral relationships must be dealt with.

Conclusion

It is critical for seminarians to know in their mind and heart whether celibate chastity is a meaningful and fulfilling way for them to live their lives as sexual beings. This goal becomes reality when they engage in a program of formation that cultivates an appreciation for the charism of celibacy, a disposition for accepting the charism, a recognition of the presence of the charism, and the practice of celibate chastity. They can then make a commitment to a life of celibate chastity that entails the renunciation of the goods of genital sexual expression, conjugal love, and natural fatherhood for the sake of the Kingdom of God. They will then experience priestly celibacy as a sign and as a motive of pastoral charity in the service of God's people.

Priestly celibacy is distinct from bachelorhood, consecrated virginity, and the religious vow of celibacy. Priestly celibacy is in service of pastoral ministry. Priestly celibacy, as with the whole of priestly identity, is ordered to and finds its fulfillment in pastoral relationships. The celibate priest is close to Christ and meets his personal needs for emotional intimacy *so that he can* serve the people, draw close to them, and draw them close to God. At the same time, the priest grows in holiness through his ministry of preaching the Word, presiding at the Eucharist and other sacraments, and pastoring the faith community. This dialectical spirituality is expressed in Vatican II. "For it is through the sacred actions they perform every day, as through their whole ministry which they exercise in union with the bishop and their fellow priests, that they are set on the right course to perfection of life. The very holiness of priests is of the greatest benefit for the fruitful fulfillment of their ministry."[126] Because celibacy is in harmony with the priesthood, it enables priests to dedicate their lives for the service of the Church more readily, more freely, and in a less encumbered way. And their ministry becomes the medium of their own ongoing conversion of mind and heart.

Celibacy is a gift given by God in the Church. It is one of many gifts and it is given to those who minister as ordained priests. It is woven into the process of the mysterious growth of the Body of Christ, the coming of the reign of God.

> And [God] gave some as apostles, others as prophets, others as evangelists,
> others as pastors and teachers, to equip the holy ones for the work of ministry,
> for building up the body of Christ, until we all attain to the unity of faith and

knowledge of the Son of God, to mature manhood, to the extent of the full stature of Christ, so that we may no longer be infants, tossed by waves and swept along by every wind of teaching arising from human trickery, from their cunning in the interests of deceitful scheming. Rather, living the truth in love, we should grow in every way into him who is the head, Christ, from whom the whole body, joined and held together by every supporting ligament, with the proper functioning of each part, brings about the body's growth and builds itself up in love (Eph 4:11-16).

May the charism of celibacy be instrumental in bringing the Church to full stature in Christ. May each priest experience himself in the celibate state as one who grows in Christ-like maturity. May the Lord who begins the good work bring it to completion.

These chapters are not meant to be an exhaustive study. Many good resources are becoming available. My goal has been to provide a "readable road map for the journey"[127] of initial and ongoing formation for priestly celibacy along with some tools and skills to reverently stir into flame the gift of God, "much as one might do with the embers of a fire, in the sense of welcoming it and living it out without ever losing or forgetting that 'permanent novelty' which is characteristic of every gift from God, who makes all things new (cf. Rev 21:5), and thus living it out in its unfading freshness and orginal beauty."[128] Such a celibate priest is like the Matthean learned scribe: "then every scribe who has been instructed in the kingdom of heaven is like the head of a household who brings from his storeroom both the new and the old" (Mt 13:52).

NOTES

[1] Pope Paul VI, *Sacerdotalis Caelibatus (On Priestly Celibacy)*, 1967, n. 1, 72, 3. The text of the encyclical appears in this book, beginning on page 97.

[2] *Presbyterorum Ordinis (Decree on the Ministry and Life of Priests)*, n. 16. This imagery is also found in *Lumen Gentium*, n. 42. All references to documents of the Second Vatican Council are from the edition by Austin Flannery, O.P., (Northport, New York: Costello Publishing Co., 1996).

[3] The names and persons described in these vignettes are fictitious. Any resemblance to actual persons is purely accidental.

[4] Sacred Congregation for Catholic Education, *A Guide to Formation in Priestly Celibacy*, 1974, n. 1.

[5] Ibid., n. 47.

[6] Ibid.

[7] Ibid., n. 17-33.

[8] All Scripture quotes are from *The New American Bible*, 1970, 1986, 1991, unless otherwise noted.

[9] A. W. Richard Sipe, *Celibacy: A Way of Loving, Living, and Serving* (Liguori, MO: Triumph Books, 1996), 79.

[10] *Program of Priestly Formation*, National Conference of Catholic Bishops, 1992, n. 267.

[11]   See Bernard R. Bonnot, "Stages in a Celibate's Life," *Human Development* 16 (Fall 1995) for a helpful article on the developmental nature of celibacy based on Erik Erikson's stages. See also A. W. Richard Sipe, *A Secret World: Sexuality and the Search for Celibacy* (New York: Brunner/Mazel, Publishers, 1990), 237-262, for another developmental schema.

[12]   Pope John Paul II, *Pastores Dabo Vobis*, The Post-synodal Apostolic Exhortation on the Formation of Priests in the Circumstances of the Present Day, 1992, n. 29.

[13]   "Statement on Celibacy."   A statement released by the National Conference of Catholic Bishops Executive Committee in the name of all the bishops, November 14, 1969, no. 20.

[14]   John McAreavey, "Celibacy: A Gift of Pastoral Charity," in *The Formation Journey of the Priest: Exploring Pastores Dabo Vobis*, ed. Bede McGregor, O.P., and Thomas Norris (Dublin: The Columba Press, 1994), 108.

[15]   *Sacerdotalis Caelibatus*, n. 72.

[16]   Pope John Paul II, *The Theology of the Body: Human Love in the Divine Plan* (Boston: Pauline Books and Media, 1997), 295.   This is part of a series of general audiences by the Holy Father in 1982.

[17]   Ibid.

[18]   Charles A. Gallagher and Thomas L. Vandenberg, *The Celibacy Myth: Loving for Life* (New York: Crossroad, 1989), 77.

[19]   Marie Theresa Coombs and Francis Kelly Nemeck, O.M.I., *Discerning Vocations to Marriage, Celibacy and Singlehood* (Collegeville: The Liturgical Press, 1994), 4.

[20]   Edward Schillebeeckx, O.P., *Celibacy* (New York: Sheed and Ward, 1968), 22-23.

[21]   Ibid., 25.

[22]   Coombs and Nemeck, 113.

[23]   Ibid.

[24]   Ibid., 115.

[25]   *Presbyterorum Ordinis*, n. 16.   See also the ordination ritual, page 77 in this book.

[26]   *Sacerdotalis Caelibatus*, n. 71.

[27]   Schillebeeckx, 124.   See pages 120-129 for his description of the fundamental archetype of the anthropological pattern at work here.

[28]   Ibid., 125-126.

[29]   Apostolic Constitution *Sacrae Disciplinae Leges* in *Code of Canon Law, Latin-English Edition* (Washington, D.C.: Canon Law Society of America, 1983), xiv.

[30]   See "Chastity," in Michael Downey, ed., *The New Dictionary of Catholic Spirituality* (Collegeville: The Liturgical Press, 1993), 147-151.

[31]   Wilkie Au, S.J., *By Way of the Heart: Toward a Holistic Christian Spirituality* (New York: Paulist Press, 1989), 141.

[32]   National Conference of Catholic Bishops, *Human Sexuality: A Catholic Perspective for Education and Lifelong Learning* (Washington, D.C.: United States Catholic Conference, 1991), 19.

[33]   Raymond J. Gunzel, *Celibacy: Renewing the Gift, Releasing the Power* (Kansas City, MO: Sheed and Ward, 1988), 9.

[34]   Ibid, 10.

[35]   Pope John Paul II, *Familiaris Consortio* (1981), no. 97.

[36]   *Human Sexuality: A Catholic Perspective for Education and Lifelong Learning*, 8-9.   The bishops cite the Congregation for Catholic Education, *Educational Guidance in Human Love* (1 November 1983), no. 4.

[37]   *Catechism of the Catholic Church* (Liguori, MO: Liguori Publications, 1994), n. 2339.

[38]   Ibid., n. 2346.

[39] Benedict J. Groeschel, O.F.M., Cap., *The Courage to Be Chaste* (New York: Paulist Press, 1985).

[40] Pope John Paul II, *The Theology of the Body*, 271.

[41] *Program of Priestly Formation*, n. 288.

[42] See Kieran Kavanaugh, O.C.D., and Otilio Rodriguez, O.C.D., trans., *The Collected Works of St. Teresa of Avila, volume one, The Book of Her Life* (Washington, D.C.: Institute of Carmelite Studies, 1987), chapters 11-21.

[43] Catherine Mowry LaCugna and Michael Downey, "Trinitarian Spirituality," in *The New Dictionary of Catholic Spirituality*, ed. Michael Downey (Collegeville: The Liturgical Press, 1993), 974.

[44] Ibid.

[45] *Pastores Dabo Vobis*, n. 12, 46.

[46] *Optatam Totius (Decree on the Training of Priests)*, n. 8.

[47] Shaun McCarty, S.T., *Partners in the Divine Dance of Our Three Person'd God* (New York: Paulist Press, 1996), 25.

[48] George E. Ganss, S.J., *The Spiritual Exercises of Saint Ignatius* (Chicago: Loyola University Press, 1992), n. 54.

[49] Henri J. M. Nouwen, *Behold the Beauty of the Lord: Praying with Icons* (Notre Dame: Ave Maria Press, 1987), 20-24.

[50] This theme runs throughout *Pastores Dabo Vobis*. See especially n. 21-23. The Holy Father echoes the teaching in *Presbyterorum Ordinis*, n. 2, 12.

[51] *Pastores Dabo Vobis*, n. 72.

[52] McAreavey, 109. See *Pastores Dabo Vobis*, n. 23.

[53] McAreavey, 109.

[54] *The Ministerial Priesthood* (1971 Synod of Bishops), in *Norms for Priestly Formation*, v. 1 (Washington, D.C.: National Conference of Catholic Bishops, 1993), 307.

[55] *Pastores Dabo Vobis*, n. 29.

[56] *Lumen Gentium*, n. 42.

[57] *Pastores Dabo Vobis*, n. 23-24. The Pope uses an image from St. Augustine: *Sit amoris officium pascere dominicum gregem.*

[58] See George Aschenbrenner, S.J., "Consciousness Examen." *Review for Religious* 31 (1972): 14-21 and David Townsend, S.J., "Finding God in a Busy Day." *Review for Religious* 50 (1991): 43-63 for helpful background material on the examen.

[59] This method was described in a course on the history and development of Ignatian spirituality taught by Fr. John Futrell, S.J., at the University of San Francisco.

[60] Gunzel, vi.

[61] A. W. Richard Sipe, *A Secret World: Sexuality and the Search for Celibacy* (New York: Brunner/Mazel, Publishers, 1990), 268. See the work sheets on pages 88-91 of this book for his schema of the interactive dynamic of the celibate person.

[62] I am indebted to Fr. John Heagle, co-director of Therapy and Renewal Associates in Seattle, Washington, for this insight.

[63] See Michael S. Driscoll, "Sexuality and Spirituality in the Life of the Celibate." *Chicago Studies* 32 (November, 1993).

[64] Sipe, *Celibacy*, 67.

[65] Kieran Kavanaugh, O.C.D., and Otilio Rodriguez, O.C.D., trans., *The Collected Works of Saint John of the Cross* (Washington, D.C.: Institute of Carmelite Studies, 1991), 52-53.

[66] Shaun McCarty, "Some Celibacy for Everyone," *Human Development* 11 (Summer, 1990): 30.

[67] Gunzel, 79-80.

[68]   Ibid., 82.

[69]   I am indebted to Dr. Gerald E. Kochansky for this insight. He was my tutor during my participation in The Christian Institute for the Study of Human Sexuality.

[70]   Gerald D. Coleman, "Celibacy Demands Grieving." *Human Development* 15 (Winter, 1994): 17-19.

[71]   Coombs and Nemeck, 110.

[72]   Sipe, *Celibacy*, 87-90.

[73]   *Program of Priestly Formation*, n. 294.

[74]   Sacred Congregation for the Doctrine of the Faith, *Declaration on Certain Questions Concerning Sexual Ethics*, December 29, 1975, no. 1.

[75]   Fran Ferder and John Heagle, *Your Sexual Self: Pathway to Authentic Intimacy* (Notre Dame: Ave Maria Press, 1992), 38.

[76]   Ibid, 44.

[77]   *A Guide to Formation in Priestly Celibacy*, n. 20.

[78]   Gerald D. Coleman, *Human Sexuality: An All-Embracing Gift* (New York: Alba House, 1992), 64.

[79]   See Coleman, *Human Sexuality*, 55-92, for a helpful discussion of these three dimensions of sexual identity.

[80]   John Money, *Lovemaps: Clinical Concepts of Sexual/Erotic Health and Pathology, Paraphilia, and Gender Transposition in Childhood, Adolescence, and Maturity* (New York: Irvington Publishers, Inc., 1986), xvi.

[81]   Edward O. Laumann, et al., *The Social Organization of Sexuality: Sexual Practices in the United States* (Chicago: The University of Chicago Press, 1994), 285.

[82]   Richard C. Friedman, *Male Homosexuality: A Contemporary Psychoanalytic Perspective* (New Haven: Yale University Press, 1988), 3, and Laumann, 291.

[83]   Friedman, 3-4.

[84]   Gerald D. Coleman, *Homosexuality: Catholic Teaching and Pastoral Practice* (New York: Paulist Press, 1995), 27.

[85]   Sipe, *A Secret World*, 139.

[86]   Laumann, 83.

[87]   Sipe, *A Secret World*, 139-158.

[88]   Eli Coleman, "Compulsion: Sexual Compulsion." in Vern L. Bullough and Bonnie Bullough, eds. *Human Sexuality: An Encyclopedia* (New York: Garland Publishing, Inc., 1994), 135.

[89]   Isidore Bernstein, "Integrative Aspects of Masturbation," in Irwin M. Marcul and John J. Francis. *Masturbation From Infancy to Senescence* (New York: International Universities Press, Inc., 1975), 62.

[90]   Vincent J. Genovesi, S.J., *In Pursuit of Love: Catholic Morality and Human Sexuality*, Second Edition (Collegeville: The Liturgical Press, 1996), 330.

[91]   See pages 314-337.

[92]   *Catechism of the Catholic Church*, n. 2352.

[93]   *Code of Canon Law*, canon 277.1.

[94]   A. W. Richard Sipe, *Sex, Priests, and Power: Anatomy of a Crisis* (New York: Brunner/ Mazel, Publishers, 1995), 18.

[95]   Sheila Murphy, *A Delicate Dance: Sexuality, Celibacy, and Relationships Among Catholic Clergy and Religious* (New York: Crossroad, 1992), 96.

[96]   Ibid., 100.

[97]   Gerald D. Coleman, S.S. "Taking a Sexual History," *Human Development* 17 (Spring, 1996): 10-15. For an even more comprehensive interview, consult the "St. Luke Institute

Psychosexual Interview," St. Luke Institute, 8901 New Hampshire Ave., Silver Spring, Maryland 20903. Phone number: 301-445-7970.

[98]   Donald J. Goergen, O.P., *The Sexual Celibate* (New York: The Seabury Press, 1974), 207.

[99]   Erik H. Erikson, *Childhood and Society*, 2nd ed. (New York: Norton, 1963), 263.

[100]   These distinctions are explored by Keith Clark, O.F.M., Cap., in an audio tape titled "The Sexuality Factor: A Key for Celibate Intimacy," (Canfield, Ohio: Alba House Cassettes, 1994).

[101]   Sean D. Sammon, *An Undivided Heart: Making Sense of Celibate Chastity* (New York: Alba House, 1993), 56-64.

[102]   *Pastores Dabo Vobis*, n. 44.

[103]   Coombs and Nemeck, 164-165. See their chapter 18, "The Expression of Celibate Love," for their helpful treatment of this topic.

[104]   This theme runs throughout Gallagher and Vandenberg's book. See especially pages 5, 15, 42, 89.

[105]   *Lumen Gentium*, n. 28. This teaching is echoed in *Presbyterorum Ordinis*, n. 6.

[106]   Ernest E. Larkin, O.Carm. "Human Relationships in Saint Teresa of Avila," in *The Land of Carmel: Essays in Honor of Joachim Smet, O.Carm.*, ed. Paul Chandler, O.Carm. and Keith J. Egan (Rome: Institutum Carmelitanum, 1991), 293.

[107]   *The Way of Perfection*, 6:3, in Kieran Kavanaugh, O.C.D. and Otilio Rodriguez, O.C.D., *The Collected Works of St. Teresa of Avila*, vol. 2 (Washington, D.C.: ICS Publications, 1980), 62. Cited by Larkin, 293.

[108]   Larkin, 295.

[109]   Ibid., 287.

[110]   *Way of Perfection*, 6:7.

[111]   Gunzel, 63-64.

[112]   Gunzel, 74.

[113]   Jane F. Becker, "Formation for Priestly Celibacy: Pertinent Issues." *Journal of Pastoral Counseling* (Spring-Summer, 1987): 72.

[114]   Becker, 73-74.

[115]   *Lumen Gentium*, n. 28.

[116]   *Presbyterorum Ordinis*, n. 8.

[117]   *Optatam Totius*, n. 11.

[118]   See Carlo Cardinal Martini, *After Some Years: Reflections on the Ministry of the Priest* (Dublin: Veritas Publications, 1991). Martini uses Acts 20 as a basis for a retreat for priests designed to bring confirmation and consolation.

[119]   Gunzel, 66.

[120]   *Sacerdotalis Caelibatus*, no. 64.

[121]   *PPF*, no. 294.

[122]   Ibid, no. 291.

[123]   Marilyn R. Peterson, *At Personal Risk: Boundary Violations in Professional-Client Relationships* (New York: W. W. Norton and Company, 1992), 76-94.

[124]   Paul B. Macke, S.J., "Boundaries in Ministerial Relationships," *Human Development* 14 (Spring, 1993): 23-24.

[125]   The expectations listed here are taken from Part IV, "Specific Behavioral Expectations" in the document titled *Formation for Celibate Chastity*. It is published by The Saint Paul Seminary School of Divinity and used in its celibacy formation program.

[126]   *Presbyterorum Ordinis*, n. 12.

[127]   A. W. Richard Sipe, "Education for Celibacy: An American Challenge." *America* (May 18, 1991), 548.

[128]   *Pastores Dabo Vobis*, n. 70.

Bibliography

Au, Wilke, S.J. *By Way of the Heart: Toward a Holistic Christian Spirituality.* New York: Paulist Press, 1989.

Clark, Keith. *An Experience of Celibacy: A Creative Reflection on Intimacy, Loneliness, Sexuality and Commitment.* Notre Dame: Ave Maria Press, 1982.

_____. *Being Sexual and Celibate.* Notre Dame: Ave Maria Press, 1986.

Coleman, Gerald D., S.S. *Human Sexuality: An All-Embracing Gift.* New York: Alba House, 1992.

_____. *Homosexuality: Catholic Teaching and Pastoral Practice.* New York: Paulist Press, 1995.

Coombs, Marie Theresa and Francis Kelly Nemeck, O.M.I. *Discerning Vocations to Marriage, Celibacy and Singlehood.* Collegeville: The Liturgical Press, 1994.

Crosby, Michael H. *Celibacy: Means of Control or Mandate of the Heart?* Notre Dame: Ave Maria Press, 1996.

Directory on the Ministry and Life of Priests. Vatican City: Congregation for the Clergy, 1994.

Ferder, Fran and John Heagle. *Your Sexual Self: Pathway to Authentic Intimacy.* Notre Dame: Ave Maria Press, 1992.

Gallagher, Charles A. and Thomas L. Vandenberg. *The Celibacy Myth: Loving for Life.* New York: Crossroad, 1989.

Genovesi, Vincent J., S.J. *In Pursuit of Love: Catholic Morality and Human Sexuality.* Second Edition. Collegeville: The Liturgical Press, 1996.

Goergen, Donald, O.P. *The Sexual Celibate.* New York: The Seabury Press, 1974.

Groeschel, Benedict J., O.F.M.Cap. *The Courage to be Chaste.* New York: Paulist Press, 1985.

A Guide to Formation in Priestly Celibacy. Vatican City: Sacred Congregation for Catholic Education, 1974.

Gunzel, Raymond J. *Celibacy: Renewing the Gift, Releasing the Power.* Kansas City: Sheed and Ward, 1988.

Huddleston, Mary Anne, I.H.M., ed. *Celibate Loving: Encounter in Three Dimensions.* New York: Paulist Press, 1984.

Human Sexuality: A Catholic Perspective for Education and Lifelong Learning. Washington, D.C.: United States Catholic Conference, 1991.

John Paul II. *I Will Give You Shepherds (Pastores Dabo Vobis): Post-Synodal Apostolic Exhortation.* Washington, D.C.: United States Catholic Conference, 1992.

_____. *The Theology of the Body: Human Love in the Divine Plan.* Boston: Pauline Books and Media, 1997.

Kiesling, Christopher, O.P. *Celibacy, Prayer and Friendship: A Making-Sense-Out-Of-Life Approach.* New York: Alba House, 1978.

Kraft, William. *Sexual Dimensions of the Celibate Life.* Kansas City: Andrews and McMeel, Inc., 1979.

McGregor, Bede, O.P. and Thomas Norris, eds. *The Formation Journey of the Priest: Exploring Pastores Dabo Vobis.* Dublin: The Columba Press, 1994.

Murphy, Sheila. *A Delicate Dance: Sexuality, Celibacy, and Relationships Among Catholic Clergy and Religious.* New York: Crossroad, 1992.

Nelson, James B. *The Intimate Connection: Male Sexuality, Masculine Spirituality.* Philadelphia: The Westminster Press, 1988.

Norms for Priestly Formation. Vol. 1 and 2. Washington, D.C.: National Conference of Catholic Bishops, 1993.

Paul VI. *Encyclical Letter on Priestly Celibacy (Sacerdotalis Caelibatus).* Washington, D.C.: Unites States Catholic Conference, 1967.

Peterson, Marilyn R. *At Personal Risk: Boundary Violations in Professional-Client Relationships.* New York: W. W. Norton and Company, 1992.

Program of Priestly Formation, Fourth Edition. Washington, D.C.: National Conference of Catholic Bishops, 1992.

A Reflection Guide on Human Sexuality and the Ordained Priesthood. Washington, D.C.: National Conference of Catholic Bishops, 1983.

Rossetti, Stephen J. *Slayer of the Soul: Child Sexual Abuse and the Catholic Church.* Mystic: Twenty-Third Publications, 1990.

Sammon, Sean D. *An Undivided Heart: Making Sense of Celibate Chastity.* New York: Alba House, 1993.

Schillebeeckx, Edward. *Celibacy.* New York: Sheed and Ward, 1968.

Sipe, A.W. Richard. *A Secret World: Sexuality and the Search for Celibacy.* New York: Brunner/Mazel, Publishers, 1990.

_____. *Sex, Priests, and Power: Anatomy of a Crisis.* New York: Brunner/Mazel, Publishers, 1995.

_____. *Celibacy: A Way of Loving, Living, and Serving.* Liguori, MO: Triumph Books, 1996.

Tyrrell, Thomas J. *Urgent Longings.* Whitinsville, MA: Affirmation Books, 1980.

Wister, Robert, ed. *Psychology, Counseling and the Seminarian.* Washington, D.C.: National Catholic Educational Association, Seminary Department, 1994.

There are numerous articles in various periodicals that deal with various aspects of sexuality and celibacy. A few of them have been cited in these chapters.

Chicago Studies devoted two issues to the topic of Sexuality and the Spiritual Life in 1993 (Vol. 32, no. 1 & 3).

Human Development regularly has articles on these subjects.

Appendices
&
Worksheets

A Program of Formation for Priestly Celibacy

What does a program of formation for priestly celibacy look like?

With the seven guiding principles in mind, the program of formation for priestly celibacy at The Saint Paul Seminary School of Divinity is comprised of the following components: community support, solitude and private prayer, a developmental formation program, individualized formation, and academic courses.

A. Community Support

The call to celibacy as a viable and life-giving way of living the Christian journey must be supported and nurtured by the ecclesial community. This happens in daily gatherings for the Liturgy and meals and in other opportunities for fellowship. Healthy and happy priests and other professed celibates provide witness and encouragement for seminarians. Gatherings in small groups in the parish and at the seminary provide opportunities for interaction and support. The wing groups on each floor of the seminary residence offer the students an experience of gathering with people who live near them for prayer and fellowship, much like the gatherings of priests in their deaneries.

B. Solitude and Private Prayer

The experience of solitude and private prayer are essential in priestly celibacy. Each seminarian's spiritual director assists him in fostering a pattern of prayer and reflection in his daily life. The Prayer Practicum in Theology I explores the rich diversity of prayer in the Christian Tradition. Students are expected to work towards spending one sustained hour in private prayer each day. Retreats and days of recollection provide blocks of time for extended periods of prayer and solitude. Students are encouraged to make use of the Pacem in Terris hermitages and other opportunities for solitude.

C. A Developmental Formation Program

A developmental program of formation for priestly celibacy is woven throughout the four years of theology in the Wednesday Morning Formation Program. Each level of theology has a minimum of three sessions of two hours duration.

Theology I: During the January Spiritual Life Practicum titled *Spirituality in Diocesan*

Priesthood, one week is devoted to an intensive program on the dynamics of human sexuality and the meaning of celibate chastity. Topics include psychosexual development, fostering sexual health, what happens when sexual health breaks down, masculinity and spirituality, and ecclesial expectations regarding sexual behavior.

Theology II: In this level of formation appropriate ways of dealing with sexual feelings and appropriate expressions of intimacy are explored. The encyclical of Pope Paul VI, *Sacerdotalis Caelibatus* is studied. Seminarians are guided in reflecting on their own rationale for making a celibate commitment. Ways of internalizing the value of priestly celibacy are explored.

Theology III: The entire Fall semester of the formation program is devoted to formation for celibate chastity. The set of six videos and printed materials titled *Men Vowed and Sexual: Conversations about Celibate Chastity* is used in their weekly meetings. The six topics are intimacy, men and women in relationship, falling in love, homosexuality, midlife and generativity, and the mystery of celibate chastity.

Theology IV: During this final year of formation, conferences deal with the human, psychological, and legal dimensions of sexual issues in ministry. Appropriate boundaries in pastoral relationships are discussed. Additionally, sessions explore the experience of priestly celibacy as an evolving and developmental process.

Human Growth Workshops: Throughout the four years of theology about fifteen hours are devoted to foundational human dynamics. These include self-esteem, dealing with anger, conflict resolution, family systems, addictions, and male identity development.

D. Individualized Formation

Spiritual Direction: Each seminarian meets bi-weekly with his spiritual director. This confidential relationship provides him with the opportunity to receive guidance in integrating his sexuality, the value of prayer and solitude, his intimacy needs, and his ability to internalize a commitment to celibate chastity. "In this setting, seminarians should be encouraged to speak in detail about their own personal struggles and review their successes and failures in living a chaste, celibate life" (*PPF*, n. 291).

Formation Advising: Each student meets twice each semester with his Formation Advisor. During these meetings he is expected to speak about his understanding of celibate chastity and his readiness for the celibate commitment. "The rector, faculty, or those charged with formation must be able to testify to seminarians' positive capacity to live a celibate life relating with others in a mature fashion or to testify to counterindicators as the case may be" (*PPF*, n. 294).

Counseling: Many students meet with a professional counselor to deal with issues about sexual identity, intimacy needs, and relationships. The Counseling Services of the University of St. Thomas provide a great resource in this area.

E. Academic Courses

The topics of celibacy and chastity are treated in various ways in the following courses:

MT701	Sexual Morality
ST600	Church Ministry and Holy Orders
PT502	Spirituality in Diocesan Priesthood
PT602	General Principles of Church Law
ST701	Christian Marriage
HS501 & 502	The History of the Christian Tradition

Ordination Ritual[1]

Commitment to Celibacy

After the homily the candidate, if he is to manifest his intention of a commitment to celibacy, stands before the bishop. The bishop speaks to him in these or similar words:

By your own free choice you seek to enter the order of deacons. You shall exercise this ministry in the celibate state for celibacy is both a sign and a motive of pastoral charity, and a special source of spiritual fruitfulness in the world. By living in this state with total dedication, moved by a sincere love for Christ the Lord, you are consecrated to him in a new and special way. By this consecration you will adhere more easily to Christ with an undivided heart; you will be more freely at the service of God and mankind, and you will be more untrammeled in the ministry of Christian conversion and rebirth. By your life and character you will give witness to your brothers and sisters in faith that God must be loved above all else, and that it is he whom you serve in others.

Therefore, I ask you:
In the presence of God and the Church, are you resolved, as a sign of your interior dedication to Christ, to remain celibate for the sake of the kingdom and in lifelong service to God and mankind?

The candidate answers:
I am.

If it wishes, the conference of bishops may determine some external sign to express the intention of the candidate.

The bishop adds:
May the Lord help you to persevere in this commitment.

The candidate answers:
Amen.

Code of Canon Law[2]

Canons Concerning Celibacy in the Code of Canon Law

Book II, Part I, Title III, Chapter I The Formation of Clerics

Canon 247.1 The students are to be prepared through suitable education to observe the state of celibacy, and they are also to learn to honor it as a special gift of God.

Canon 247.2 They are to be duly informed of the duties and burdens of sacred ministers of the Church; no difficulty of priestly life is to be kept back from them.

Book II, Part I, Title III, Chapter III The Obligations and Rights of Clerics

Canon 277.1 Clerics are obliged to observe perfect and perpetual continence for the sake of the kingdom of heaven and therefore are obliged to observe celibacy, which is a special gift of God, by which sacred ministers can adhere more easily to Christ with an undivided heart and can more freely dedicate themselves to the service of God and humankind.

Canon 277.2 Clerics are to conduct themselves with due prudence in associating with persons whose company could endanger their obligation to observe continence or could cause scandal for the faithful.

Canon 277.3 The diocesan bishop has the competence to issue more specific norms concerning this matter and to pass judgement in particular cases concerning the observance of this obligation.

Book II, Part III, Section I, Title I Norms Common To All Institutes of Consecrated Life

Canon 599 The evangelical counsel of chastity assumed for the sake of the kingdom of heaven, as a sign of the future world and a source of more abundant fruitfulness in an undivided heart, entails the obligation of perfect continence in celibacy.

Definition of Celibacy

In his books, *A Secret World: Sexuality and the Search for Celibacy* (p. 58) and *Celibacy: A Way of Loving, Living, and Serving* (p. 40), A. W. Richard Sipe defines celibacy this way:

> Celibacy is a freely chosen dynamic state, usually vowed, that involves an honest and sustained attempt to live without direct sexual gratification in order to serve others productively for a spiritual motive.

How would you modify this definition?

What are your reasons for your revisions?

The Five C's

Describe the meaning and role of each of these terms in the experience of priestly celibacy.

1. **Celibacy**

2. **Chastity**

3. **Continence**

4. **Conscience**

5. **Charity**

Why Celibacy for Me?

Priestly celibacy must become "the candidate's own accepted personal obligation under the influence of divine grace and with full reflection and liberty" (*Sacerdotalis Caelibatus* # 72). The following is a list of various motives for embracing a life of celibate chastity. Given your experience, prayer, study, and reflection, how would you articulate your own rationale for celibacy? How does celibacy make sense for you? Why do you want to be celibate?

1. Commitment of the total self to the proclamation of the Kingdom of God.

2. Being a prophetic countercultural sign of the reign of God, thereby inviting all people to ask questions about the ultimate meaning of life.

3. A requirement of Church law demanding obedience.

4. Embracing celibacy as imitation of Christ by sharing in his very condition of living.

5. A deep interior sense of being personally called by God to live as a celibate.

6. An expression of the cross and the paschal mystery — life-giving self denial.

7. Freedom to belong to a community larger than the blood family (fraternity of priests, religious community, parish, global Church).

8. An emptying of self that is also a way of yielding a space of hospitality for God and other people (friends, parishioners, the poor).

9. It provides for the experience of a spousal relationship with God.

10. Celibacy is a way of loving and a way of being life-giving that is meaningful and attractive to me.

11. I experience celibacy as a charism, a gift from God, a graced way of being.

12. A state of life that allows more freedom and availability for pastoral relationships.

13. Celibate chastity is a fulfilling way for me to live my life as a sexual being.

14. It is a way of living that anticipates all creation's full union with Jesus Christ in the new world of the future resurrection.

15. A complex eclectic tapestry that is largely a mystery

Seven Ways of Dealing with Sexual Feelings

1. Denial: refusal to admit that certain facts or actions exist; often a rejection of obvious evidence. This denial often occurs in interpersonal and social situations.

2. Repression: an intrapsychic process, an unconscious coping mechanism. Repression entails not being conscious of one's experiences of sexual feelings and not being consciously aware of being unaware.

3. Sexual acting out: engaging in genital behavior with others or with oneself that includes oral, vaginal, and anal intercourse, foreplay, and masturbation.

4. Expression: to make known or communicate one's experience of sexual feelings. Expression includes "self-talk," journaling, and talking to another appropriate person, for example, a friend, confidant, or spiritual director.

5. Suppression: a conscious coping mechanism that entails the awareness and acceptance of sexual feelings and choosing not to promote them or act on them.

6. Sublimation: the process of awareness and acceptance of sexual feelings and channeling the sexual energy to activity judged to be "higher" culturally, socially, physically, aesthetically, or spiritually.

7. Respectful integration:[3] a direct way of integrating sexual feelings and spirituality to foster religious growth. In respectful integration a person looks in love at sexual feelings as an opportunity to see the whole person (oneself and others).

Reflection on Sexuality Continuum

Looking at the continuum on page 71, where does it seem I live most of the time?

At the left: (Non-assertive sexuality)

Do I bury myself in work and have less intimacy than I need?

Do I accomplish goals but offer less personal, deep human contact than I could?

Am I uncomfortable with affection from women or from men?

Am I ill at ease in my body and troubled and anxious about my sexuality?

Do I feel noticeably awkward around women or men? Hostile?

Do I let others manipulate me sexually, somehow not saying "No" when I want to?

Am I lonely a good part of the time?

Are there other thoughts or behaviors that struck home with me about this side of the continuum?

In the center: (Assertive sexuality)

Am I comfortable with my body and its power, with my sexuality and its life?

Am I open with myself about my genitality and compassionate with myself about the difficulties of celibacy in this area?

Am I at ease with both men and women, working, playing, exchanging appropriate affection, sharing at deep emotional and spiritual levels when it is fitting?

Do I have close friends I can really share with?

Do I know how to reflect and choose what fits for me sexually?

Do I know how to say "No" kindly but confidently?

Are there other thoughts and behaviors that struck home with me about this side of the continuum?

At the right: (Aggressive sexuality)

Do I flaunt my sexuality? Play on the emotions of others without taking into consideration the effect on them?

Do I move into the emotional life of others without any commitment to them?

Do I exploit (get my needs met without giving in return) others without taking responsibility for it?

Do I "collect" admirers? Feel unsafe if there are not several people who are a little "hooked on" me?

Do I have physicality in my life that does not fit at all?

Do I act out my negative feelings about people by being hostile, controlling or cold?

Area there other thoughts and behaviors that struck home with me about this side of the continuum?

© Patricia H. Livingston, Livingston Associates, 2 Adalia Avenue #501, Tampa FL 33606

Continuum of Human Sexuality

	Non-Assertive	Assertive	Aggressive
	Low Self-Esteem	High Self-Esteem	Low Self-Esteem
	little or no sense of sexual power – repressed or unclaimed	aware of power, integrating it, exercising it lovingly	preoccupied by power, using it on others, overpowering
Primary Sexuality (feelings about body, about self as man or woman)	uncomfortable with body, shy, embarrassed, awkward	comfortable with body	preoccupied with body; vain
	does not feel attractive as man or woman, does not work toward it	sees self as attractive, enjoys being a man or woman; dresses becomingly vital, graceful	Flaunts physical attractiveness; Dress emphasizes this
Genital Sexuality (gential aspect of sexuality)	afraid of stirrings, urges, desires, physical reactions; insecure about exercising this aspect of sexuality	accepting and welcoming of genitality as part of self; exercises it appropriately	flaunts genital sexuality; exploits others, seduces; insecure, need to prove potency
Affective Sexuality (ability to feel close and express closeness; ability to touch)	devoid of warmth (deadness, coldness, stereotyped role behavior)	warm and caring, able to express feelings	Aggressive warmth, invasive liveliness
	dependence on others (clinging) or on substitute substance (alcohol, food, drugs)	interdependence	fierce independence (controls with coldness, manipulation, power games such as RAPO)
	no tactility, awkward; afraid to be close	able to touch appropriately, express feelings with touch	exploits tactility and physically (passes)
	OR		
(Boundaries)	allows self to be used, doesn't defend boundary; or unaware of boundaries	own boundaries thought thru; assertive about own, and respectful of others; talk about them early in relationships where appropriate	boundaries of others are unimportant; may look on other as boundary-less possession fierce sensitivity about own

2 Adalia Avenue #501, Tampa, FL 33606

Circles of Relationships In A Priest's Life[4]

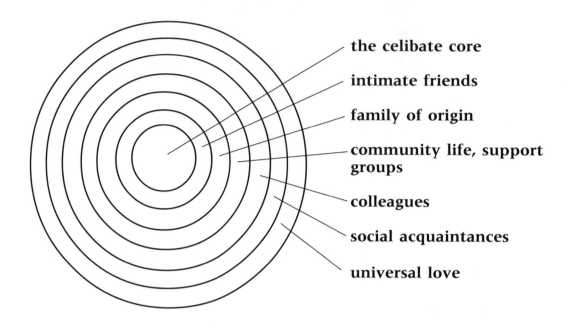

the celibate core

intimate friends

family of origin

community life, support groups

colleagues

social acquaintances

universal love

This is a possible schema to highlight the various circles of relationships in the celibate priest's life. Which persons or groups of persons will be in which circle will vary among priests and among seminarians. For example, family of origin may be closer to the center for some and may be non-existent for others.

1. How would your scheme of circles of relationships look? Name the persons you would put in the various circles.

2. Which circle(s) of relationships receive(s) most of your time and energy?

3. What does this tell you about your values and priorities?

4. Do you feel drawn to change the amount of time you spend with people within a particular circle?

Reflecting On Relational Development[5]

1. Identify early messages, spoken or unspoken, that you received about relationships, sexuality, and celibacy. What do you carry with you today from these messages? What do you want to change? What resources are available to help you?

2. How did your parents relate with each other when you were a child? How did they relate with you? What did you learn from them about relationships?

3. Reflect on your history of relationships. Which ones have been significant for you? What has been good in those relationships? What patterns can you identify that have not been helpful in relating with others?

4. In what ways is a relationship different for you when you have romantic feelings toward that person? How do your romantic notions about relationships impact your ability to relate with people?

5. How accepting and comfortable are you with your sexual orientation? With which gender are you most comfortable? Why?

6. What are your limits or boundaries regarding touch, affection, time, and place with friends? What are the signals that indicate the limits of your comfort zone? How do you respond to them?

7. Do any of your personal behaviors court accusations of scandal? How are you able to respect and accommodate the ethics and customs of your local community?

8. In what ways are you accountable to yourself, others, and God about what you are thinking, feeling, and doing as you relate with other people? With whom do you speak about concerns and limits in relationships?

NOTES

[1]   Ordination of a Deacon. *The Rites of the Catholic Church*, vol. 2 (New York: Pueblo Publishing Co., 1980), 52-53.

[2]   *The Code of Canon Law. Latin-English Edition* (Washington, D.C.: Canon Law Society of America, 1983).

[3]   William F. Kraft, "Celibate Genitality," in *Celibate Loving: Encounters in Three Dimensions*, ed. Mary Huddleston, I.H.M. (New York: Paulist Press, 1984), 85-90.

[4]   This worksheet is inspired by a similar one titled "Circles of Relationships in a Celibate's Life" by Brother James Zullo, Ph.D., used by the Center for Continuing Formation In Ministry at Notre Dame.

[5]   Adapted from a set of questions by Sheila Murphy in *A Delicate Dance: Sexuality, Celibacy, and Relationships Among Catholic Clergy and Religious* (New York: Crossroad, 1992), 111-112.

Epilogue

Celibacy: A Way to Love

Most Rev. Harry J. Flynn, D.D.
Archbishop of St. Paul and Minneapolis

This address was delivered by Archbishop Flynn, a papally appointed delegate, during the October 6 session of the 1990 Synod of Bishops. He was bishop of Lafayette, Louisiana, at that time. As a result of this worldwide synod, Pope John Paul II promulgated <u>I Will Give You Shepherds (Pastores Dabo Vobis)</u>, the post-synodal apostolic exhortation on the formation of priests in the circumstances of the present day, on March 25, 1992. The Archbishop's address is reprinted here with his permission.

CELIBACY: A WAY TO LOVE

The noted English writer, C. S. Lewis, once remarked that if you asked 20 good men of our time what they considered the highest of Christian virtues, 19 of them would likely say it was unselfishness. But if you asked the Christians of old, almost all of them would have said it was love (cf. his essay "The Weight of Glory"). The positive value of love is often overshadowed by the negative aspect of self-denial. Love focuses on the active virtue of reaching out to share the good with others, while unselfishness tends to point to our own self-abnegation.

There is a parallel to this in our image of celibacy. We often see celibacy in the solely negative terms of self-denial, whereas St. Paul saw it as a virtue in which the unmarried person "can devote himself to the Lord's affairs" (I Cor 7:32). To please the Lord is to keep His commandments, the greatest of which are to love God above all things and to love one's neighbor as oneself (Mk 12:29-30). If celibacy is a way of devoting oneself "to the affairs of the Lord," then it must be a way of loving. Indeed, celibacy is a love "which knows no rivals and a joyous disposition of heart for pastoral service" (*Instrumentum Laboris*, 35).

Yet there are many, within the Church and without, who see celibacy as a harsh form of self-denial imposed by the Church on those who want to serve as priests. Often celibacy is seen as an added burden and not as a positive and fruitful way of enhancing one's devotion to the Lord's affairs.

This sad outlook is based not only on an exclusively negative definition of celibacy; it also stems from an erroneous notion about the vocation to celibacy. Celibacy is not simply a condition necessary for priestly ordination; rather, celibacy and priesthood are two distinct though related vocations. Those who feel God is calling them to priesthood must also detect a call to celibacy. Like all vocations, both celibacy and priesthood begin with an inner desire or aspiration for priestly service which must in turn be confirmed by the Church. Please allow me to explain this latter point more fully.

All vocations begin with what I call "inspiration," the subjective element of desire. An individual may experience a feeling, perhaps a longing, which he interprets as God's call. If a vocation is to be more than a private aspiration, however, it must be confirmed.

A vocation to priesthood begins as an "inspiration," a deep desire to serve the Church as an ordained minister. It may be planted by loving parents, good priests and the gentle movement of God's grace. It may also spring from other sources such as romantic idealism or the desire for respect from others. Seminary authorities must work with the candidate to identify the source of such "inspiration." It is a process of careful discernment and patient prayer. What the candidate senses internally must receive external confirmation in the seminary. If his desire to serve comes from God, then the candidate will confirm this by his growing sense of peace, his deepening prayer and his ever deeper love for God and his Church. But there is still more.

In the end, he must present himself to his bishop, with the approval of God's people, so as to be called to holy orders. It is his own bishop, in the visible, structured church, who must finally call him for it is that church's ministry which the candidate desires to exercise. The Church's call is the final confirmation that one's desire to serve is no longer merely internal.

The Church has every right to set clear conditions for entry into priestly service — conditions of health, intelligence, education, good will, solid spiritual life. One who does not fulfill those conditions does not have this vocation. The conditions must be clear, the formation must be proper and the candidate must be honest about himself. Only then is his initial "inspiration" confirmed as a vocation.

For much of the Church, celibacy has long been a requirement for priestly ordination. The man who seeks confirmation of his priestly vocation must also be able to say in all honesty, that he has discerned in himself both the "inspiration" and the confirmation of a vocation to the celibate life.

The call to celibacy also begins from within. Its hallmark is the dedication that commits one so deeply to a mission that no room will be left for a further commitment to marriage and family. It is authentic only when it is a positive commitment to a goal, not merely the desire to set something aside as a penance. Still less is it a way of escaping personal difficulties. Fear of responsibility, aversion to sex, an incapacity to love deeply, the mere lack of opportunity — none of these are valid foundations for the vocation to celibacy. Indeed, the best qualities that one finds in a married man should also be characteristic of a celibate. Since the qualities that make for a happy marriage and a happy celibacy are so similar, individuals who feel they are called to celibacy may go through the deepest soul-searching and doubts in the process of discernment.

No one should make this commitment to a permanent celibate life simply as an act of willful self-denial or as a mere condition for ordination. Defining celibacy only as giving up sex is just as unrealistic as seeing marriage as giving up all other women. Neither marriage nor celibacy is livable without a commitment of love so deep as to cause one to want to give up all else.

Those who see the vocation to priesthood solely as in internal call will be likely to view the Church's requirement of celibacy as an unjust imposition. Some complain that they are called to priesthood, but not to celibacy. They forget that while the aspiration for priesthood begins from within, God's call comes through the call of the bishop. Without this call there is no vocation.

The fact is that the Church does not impose celibacy on priests. It cannot do so. With St. Paul we must affirm that celibacy is a gift from God that must be freely accepted (cf. I Cor. 7:7-9). Quite rightly, however, the Church does set conditions prior to calling a man to holy orders. Among them is the stipulation of a free and full commitment to a life of celibacy. In relation to orders, this commitment is *ante factum*, not *post factum*. Since 1981, the Church has required that a man state in writing that he has freely chosen celibacy. The candidate who desires to be a priest but does not have the call to celibacy does not — in the present discipline — have the call to priesthood.

In most of the society in which we live, celibacy is now, more than ever before, viewed as a sign of contradiction. It is viewed with suspicion, lack of understanding and even hostility — but it is a sign. It is "an authentic prophetic testimony in the world today" (*Instrumentum Laboris*, 38). It bears witness to the reality of Christian love and its distinctiveness from sexual expression, just as Christian marriage is a sign of the sacredness of sexuality as an expression of love.

Failures in living out celibacy attract much attention. Some see the abolition of the celibate priesthood as the solution to those difficulties, but that is no solution any more than abolishing marriage is a solution to infidelity or divorce.

The real problem is an inability to make a full and permanent commitment, a failure to grasp the reality of God's love, and a lack of solid formation so necessary to live celibacy.

How do seminaries and houses of formation teach and form men to accept and live the gift of celibacy throughout their lives? An ancient axiom of theology and spirituality tells us that "grace builds on nature." In forming men for celibacy, we need to respect what is authentically human. In that spirit, let me propose seven elements of formation for celibacy:

1. Seminary formation must, from its earliest stages, present a clear and positive concept of the vocation to priesthood and the vocation to celibacy. A recent study done in the United States of priests ordained five to nine years indicated, among other things, that most priests feel that the seminary did not discuss celibacy frankly or deeply enough. Only by presenting both priesthood and celibacy in their full reality can candidates for orders come to the point of making a free and generous response to God's call.

2. The seminarian must be required to see a well-trained and approved spiritual director at least once a month. The seminarian must be totally honest with

his spiritual director. Problems regarding chastity must be discussed with candor and, ultimately, in God's grace they must be overcome. The director must help the seminarian understand chaste celibacy as a way of love and assist him in developing habits of mind and heart that will sustain the future priest in this life-giving commitment. Indeed, every priest must be convinced of the necessity of regular spiritual direction for living a chaste, celibate life.

3. Men must be taught through workshops and conferences and in private direction that the reality of celibacy for the kingdom is far removed from the present ideals of the world. The commitment to celibacy can only be sustained in prayer. The noise of the world must be regularly shut out so as to create an island of silence where the priest or seminarian can hear the Lord speak. Candidates must be taught the absolute necessity of sustained and solitary prayer, so vital for deepening one's relationship with Christ. In those times of prayer, the Lord will chasten and he will affirm, but without it the light of celibacy is gradually extinguished.

4. Men must be taught the need for good priest friends. Here I am not speaking of group affection that can develop so easily among larger groups of priests but rather those priest friends with whom we can share our deepest selves and still experience acceptance and encouragement to live the celibate commitment. John Henry Newman once stated that the reason there were so few saints is that there were so few with whom the secrets of the heart could be shared. Priests falter in celibacy when they fail to share what is in their heart with solid and compassionate priest friends.

5. Our young men in seminaries need to be taught the value of solitude; they must learn how to be in silence so as to allow God's word to resound in their hearts. Blaise Pascal once observed, "Man's unhappiness arises from one thing only — namely, that he cannot abide quietly in one room." Candidates for the priesthood must learn to let the voice of solitude be heard and not run from that voice even if, at times, it will speak of one's own wretchedness and poverty.

6. Priestly candidates must learn now to develop a healthy sense of what they can accomplish in God's grace. They must learn to sense how they can touch and transform the lives of others with God's love. They must sense how they can build up the Church. When priests feel their work is futile, celibacy becomes more difficult to sustain.

7. Finally, the importance of self-discipline should be stressed. Candidates should be moderate in what they eat and drink; they need to follow a regular schedule and be attentive to their duties. They should learn to set aside time for exercise. The anonymous author of the 14th-century work, *The Cloud of Unknowing*, wisely observed: "This work (contemplation and love of God) demands great serenity, an integrated disposition in soul and in body. So for the love of God, tend your body and your soul alike and stay as fit as you can."

In the end, the love we offer to others is not just our own; that would be too shallow and would only lead to discouragement and failure. It must be God's love, living in and through us. Only then does celibacy become the sign God meant it to be.